The Moving Message

By Dirk Miedema

Warning!
The material in this book is very direct in nature. It has been known to instill guilt in some preachers, the author included. Therefore, it is important to take this book in combination with the full measure of God's grace in Jesus Christ.

Fairway Press
Lima, Ohio

THE MOVING MESSAGE

FIRST EDITION

7780 / ISBN 1-55673-344-5

PRINTED IN U.S.A.

Acknowledgements

My greatest gratitude is to the Triune God, who created me, saved me, sustains me and continues to perfect me.

My second debt of gratitude goes to my life partner Grace Kloosterman Miedema whose participation in my life personifies the old Freisan proverb: *"Wez in sinnestriel in oar hat'er forlet fan."*

I wish also to express my deep appreciation to Dr. Jay Adams whose well structured Doctor Ministry Program at Westminster Theological Seminary in Escondido California provided the occasion for me to write this book.

I also owe a deep debt of gratitude to Mr. Fred DeVries who out of pure Christian brotherly love overhauled the spelling, style and grammar of this book not once, but twice. I would be ashamed to put this book in print if it were not for him.

Also, I express my gratitude to the twenty-five pastors who willingly functioned as "guinea pigs" for the preaching approach described in this book, and then sent me their helpful suggestions and revisions. Thank you, as well, to Dr. C. Kromminga, and Rev. Wilbert M. Van Dyk of Calvin Theological Seminary, and Dr. William McRae of Ontario Theological Seminary who reviewed the entire book for me. Also, thank you to Dr. Howard Smick of Gordon-Conwell Seminary and Dr. Dennis Johnson of Westminster Seminary in California for reviewing selected portions.

Last, but not least thanks to the Council of Beth-El Christian Reformed Church in Acton, Ontario. They gave me the extra time I needed to complete this work.

Table of Contents

Foreword

The Moving Message by Dr. Dirk Miedema has to do with structure in preaching. That is not an altogether intriguing subject, I'll admit it. But Miedema makes it interesting — and shows it is vital.

As the title indicates, Miedema is not interested in structure of steel, stone or wood; he shows you how to use structure that moves. It is a dynamic structure that he advocates — structure that moves your message in order to move your congregation.

The book is stimulating and will make you consider (or reconsider) many of your present practices. Indeed, it may be just the breeze you need to waft you out of the doldrums on your way toward more effective preaching.

You may not agree with all you read, but you should do yourself the favor of reading. Miedema contends that the much laughed at three-point sermon outline is "best" after all (read and see if you agree). He thinks sermon forms should follow the outline of the text (should they?). And he provides the reader with a workbook in the examples; I suppose I dare not mention more (you'll have to read them for yourself!).

Jay E. Adams, 1991
Harrison Bridge Road
Presbyterian Church
Simpsonville, South Carolina

Preface

This book is not for those who consider themselves to be exceptionally gifted preachers. Rather, it is written by a struggler for strugglers. As a modestly talented pastor of a local church who often has to prepare two sermons a week, I have had my share of battles in sermon preparation. This book is the outcome of my struggles.

After almost 10 years in the ministry, I can say sermon preparation does get easier, but it remains a weekly battle royale. But, I love being a preacher! If the Lord grants me health and life, I hope to spend the rest of my life doing it!

I have to agree with Spurgeon, who also had a great love for preaching, when he said, "The quarry of the Holy Scripture is inexhaustible. I seem hardly to have begun to labor in it; but the selection of the next block, and the consideration as to how to work it into form, are matters not so easy as some think."*

Because preaching is hard work, and because it is my personal conviction that preaching is a pastor's primary task, and just because I love preaching, I have set out to systematically develop the gifts that God has given me. This book outlines the process by which I go about sermon preparation. I hope it may in some way help you in the calling that is both a struggle and blessing.

*Paul Lee Tan, *Encyclopedia of 7700 Illustrations* , (Rockville, Maryland: Assurance Publishers, 1979), p. 188.

Introduction

At an important part in your Sunday morning message, Mrs. Maclean gets up from her pew near the front of the sanctuary. As she leaves everyone wonders why. No one hears another word of your sermon. The "dynamo" has just been sucked out of your message!

What has distracted your congregation? There are at least three principles at work.

The first is movement. The eye and the mind are drawn to movement. That is why your audience's mind is drawn from your message to Mrs. Maclean's exit. So the trick is to create movement to hold the attention of your congregation. That can be done by arm waving and other pulpit dramatics, which is a good thing for any speaker to develop. My concern in this book, however, is not to teach you how to develop pulpit theatrics. Rather, I want to show you how to weave movement into the structure of the message itself.

The second principle is to tie your movement to a specific person. The movement in the sanctuary is focused on Mrs. Maclean. To compete, you must personalize your message by addressing it to those who are more important to the hearers than Mrs. Maclean; the hearers themselves. A more personalized message grabs the attention of the audience.

The third factor is inquisitiveness. As Mrs. Maclean leaves, your audience is curious, "Where is she going? Why is she leaving?" When people see movement, one of the first things they want to know is "Why?" People are naturally curious. They want to know the purpose and destination of the movement. A moving message creates the same inquisitiveness and speaks to it.

A moving message then must be active, personal, and purposeful.

My purpose in this book is to teach you how to structure moving messages. With an active, personal, and purposeful sermon you will hold your congregation's attention.

If you grasp the principles and follow the directions in this book, you will be making messages that are going somewhere — and taking people with them!

Chapter One

A Moving Message Needs A Simple Structure

I. The Need for Structure

All preachers probably need to wind down after preaching. You have your own special ways of doing so. One technique I sometimes use to wind down is what, for lack of a better word, I call "brain blasting." (I don't intend to defend the sanctity of this method of relieving tensions. But, I use it when I have the opportunity, especially after spending a Sunday as a guest preacher at a congregation some distance from my home.)

After completing the second service and bidding my farewells, I jump in my car, rev up the engine, and crank up the volume on the radio. The dial is usually set at a station that plays music by Anne Murray, Kenny Rogers, Gordon Lightfoot, The Beatles, and occasionally Elton John. They all have a chance at blasting my brain with their familiar songs. Sometimes I shout and sing along. It may be hard to picture a preacher jiving to pop music as he's traveling home from a busy Sunday, but it's my way of winding down.

What amazes me about these songs is that in the 1990s, music that was written 15, 20, or even 25 years ago can be blasting my brain. The music I grew up with as a teenager is still the main musical diet on the radio today.

New sounds since the 1960s and early 70s haven't taken hold with the audiene. One of the top radio stations in Toronto tried in vain to market the music of the late 1970s and 1980s. That music, known as "heavy metal" or "acid rock," had very little structure. Although it drew some attention, it didn't have the lasting quality of songs from the previous decade and a half. So, the radio station changed its format to the 'golden oldies' and now its audience has dramatically increased.

In almost every sphere of communication, a similiar process has taken place. For a few years the abstract and bizarre drew attention, but it received no lasting appreciation.

Abstract art was "in" for a short time and while it can still be found in art galleries, it has quickly lost its mass appeal. The centuries old art work of a Rembrandt and a Michelangelo has the greatest following today. And today's most popular work is also much more structured and distinct. Robert Bateman's wildlife drawings are drawing more attention than the abstract art by people whose names I can no longer even remember.

This period of "abstraction" has also influenced preaching. For a while, structured styles of preaching were ridiculed because many thought emphasis on structure stifled creativity in speaking. Preachers tried to escape from traditional pattern and rational designs. This, of course came quite naturally to them. But this dabbling in the eccentric was disastrous for the person in the pew. As George E. Sweazey says, "It has attracted some attention but not many hearers."[1]

It is structured music, art and preaching that gets heard and remembered.

II. Structure Is Needed To Create And Stimulate Movement

Good art, good music, and good preaching have one thing in common. They move you, which is what they are intended to do. They are meant to create a response in you. Heavy metal music creates an impression, but it does not move you. Similarly, abstract art creates a sensation but it is not moving. So also, the most moving messages are those with a plan and deliberate structure. Abstract, unorganized sermons may create an impression (usually a negative one) but they rarely move people's hearts, hands and feet.

The most moving tunes, art forms and preaching styles are those that have structure to them.

III. The Need For A Simple Structure

It is possible, however, to overdo structure by making sermons too elaborate and complex. A message must have a simple structure, so that it can be digested by almost anyone. When it becomes complicated, people throw up their hands and give up.

You have all had the exprience, I'm sure, of giving people directions when they are lost. If there are a number of ways to go, you point them to the simplest route. That is a general rule to keep in mind for preaching.

Complicated structure, like no structure at all, may create an impression but it is likely to leave your audience head spinning. A tornado has elaborate structure. But, when it strikes home it creates just one big blur, leaves everyone spinning and results in a big mess. It moves too much in too many directions! A moving message of the right sort must be simple or it will blur the listener's understanding, put him into a spin and leave his mind a mess.

IV. The Further Benefits Of Structure

A. Benefits To The Preacher

1. Structure stimulates your creative ability.

If a painter mixes all his colors together, then he has little left for creativity. But if he starts with a pallet of paints, he can blend and contrast colors. So it is with sermon construction. If you just throw your thoughts together and mix them into a weird concoction, you won't have much left to be creative. But by organizing your thoughts into separate units, you have handles to steer your moving message.

2. Structure "ups" the efficiency of your sermon preparation.

a. It improves the efficiency of collecting sermonic material. With a clear format that outlines distinct thoughts, you can easily assemble illustrative material to explain your points. An outline gives you a shopping list of items to look for.

b. It makes sermon improvement more efficient. When everything is in disarray, it is hard to know where to begin improving your message. Clear structure points out the places where the sermon needs help, so correcting and improving can be effective.

c. It helps you put the emphasis where you want it. With a set structure, you can easily focus your message and change it, if necessary. By structuring a message, you can make the parts of the sermon flow to the main point. It helps you plan sermons for logical and psychological effect.

3. Structure improves delivery.

A clear structure helps the preacher remember the message and communicate it to the people. For the first seven years of my ministry, I was a manuscript preacher reading my sermons word for word to the congregation. One of the things that freed me from the manuscript was a solid structure. I never thought I would see the day that I could preach from only an outline, but praise God the day has come!

B. Benefits To The Listener

1. Structure makes the sermon intelligible.

Structured messages are easy to grasp. It is hard to grab hold of a piece of Jello because it is a "glibberish glob." It is simpler to hold a triangular piece of pie, a rectangular brownie or a round cookie. In the same way, a structured message can be grasped by the listener.

2. Structure helps the listener remember.

A structured message is a lot like a square meal of meat, potatoes and vegetables that sticks to your ribs and stays with you for a while. It's not like quickly-melting Jello that makes little or no impact on the body.

Structure puts things in tidy packages that can be stored in our minds and unwrapped when the information is needed.

3. Structure gives the message in chunks that the listener can chew.

Sweazey says, "An audience needs definite segments, like innings in a baseball game, the pieces in a concert, or the acts in a play. It's a weary road that has no mileposts. There is rhythm in listening. If the preacher does not provide for it they will make their own."[2] Gerhard Aho says that the average attention span of a hearer is no longer than three to five minutes.[3] An outline sets out thought units between which the audience can momentarily relax.

4. Structure gives the hearer the confidence that your sermons are going somewhere and encourages him to listen.

In the introduction, I mentioned how the congregation's attention was drawn to Mrs. Maclean leaving the church. As she left, they wondered where she was going. After the service, they may still have been wondering. But, the congregation shouldn't be wondering where you were going. If your sermons cause that, your people will give up listening to you in the future. But, if you are a structured preacher your listeners will know you are going somewhere in your sermons, and they will consider it worthwhile to stick with you every time.

C. Benefits to God

A disorganized message makes God look "stupid." You are bringing a message from God to his people and how you deliver that message reflects on God, whether you like it or not. It will seem that God is as vague and mixed up as you. A lack of clarity may make a seeker think the Christian faith is not worth investigating. You owe it to God to present his wonderful gospel message as clearly as possible. The One who died on the cross for you deserves at least that much from you.

---

1. George E. Sweazey, *Preaching The Good News*, (Englewood Cliffs, New Jersey: Prentice-Hall, Inc., 1976), p. 70

2. Sweazey, *Preaching The Good News*,p. 73

3. Gerhard Aho, *The Lively Skeleton: Thematic Approaches and Outlines*, (St. Louis: Concordia Publishing, 1977), p. 70

What follows in this book is one method of structuring gospel messages that will move the heads, hearts, hands and feet of your listeners.

Chapter Two

The Main Movement

I. Preliminary Matters

Delayed once for several hours in the town of Dijon in France, I went into the venerable cathedral there. What I remember now about the cathedral is the finely wrought stone pulpit, and just beneath it the figure of a recording angel, holding a tablet in one hand and a pen in the other, with face turned upward toward the pulpit, waiting to hear and record what the preacher says.

Always the angel stands below our pulpits. He is not waiting to write down things the congregation might like to record — in pleasure or displeasure — but whether or not the words of the preacher are true to the gospel with which he has been entrusted.[1]

Macartney's words illustrate my theology of preaching. Preaching is not standing up and declaring one's own opinions. People get bombasted with opinions on daily basis. What they hear on Sunday should be different. And preaching is not giving people what they like. Often the things you like best, such as candies and other junk food, are not good for you. Preaching is giving the people an authoritative message from God's Word, the Bible, "whose bud may have a bitter taste but sweet will be the flower."

This book, is founded on a firm and unyielding commitment to expository preaching. If you are not devoted to such a philosophy of preaching, I hope this book will not help you prepare for your kind of preaching. Through this book I desire to help those who are committed to proclaiming a message that is firmly rooted in the inspired Word of God.

A more technical definition of expository preaching than my intial illustration is provided by Haddon W. Robinson. "Expository preaching is the communication of a biblical concept, derived from and transmitted through a historical, grammatical, and literary study of a passage in its context, which the Holy Spirit first applies to the personality and experience of the preacher, then through him to his hearers."[2]

The only problem that I have with this definition is the word "concept." I believe that preaching must communicate more than a concept, it should communicate what I have called "a main movement." The main movement's definition will be the subject of this chapter.

There is another preliminary matter. Just because this book deals with the nuts and bolts of preparing a structured sermon that doesn't mean that is the beginning of the whole process. I assume you are already a serious student of the Bible, and that you have done the necessary exegesis and background study to be able to write down in one, clear sentence, the central message of the scripture portion.* This book starts after all the important preliminary work has been done. It takes the raw material extracted from such a study and helps you form it into a moving message. The first and most important stage in this process is the creation of the main movement.

II. Not A Staccato Of Insights But One Main Movement

The late Dutch homiletician Klaas Dijk in his book *De Dienst Der Prediking* explains how many preachers have adopted an Abrahamic approach to preaching.[3] Like Abraham, who heard the call to leave his own country and went out not knowing where he was going, so also many preachers who hear the call stand at the pulpit not knowing where they are going. They

---

*In Appendix I you will find a brief description of how to come to such an understanding of the text.

just start, take a series of journeys, and only the Lord knows where they will end up.

Dijk points to two approaches to preaching in his day that follow this pattern. One takes a given text and explains it word for word. This, he says, amounts to no more than a staccato-like word study that ends up no where. By chopping up the Bible passage it fails to communicate the whole thought.

The second, often used when preaching on narrative passages, follows the story play by play, dispensing small gems of insight along the way. Dijk says that this too violates the overall intention of the text. Such sermons may offer a nice series of insights, but they fail to communicate God's overall message. Again, the effect is staccato-like.

Neither method is acceptable. Instead, as Dijk says, the proper approach to preaching begins with the major thought of a text which is developed through the material provided in the passage. Sermons are not simple word studies or bits of insight but are flowing messages that communicate the major thrust of the text.

III. The Difference Between A Theme and A Main Movement

Dijk espouses the thematic approach to preaching in which the preacher assesses the major thought of the text and expounds on that theme according to the information given in the text. In this book, the approach to preaching is basically the same — with modifications.

Rather than beginning with a theme or central idea or a concept, I wish to start out with something called a main movement. A main movement is a full sentence statement (complete with subject, verb and object) that differs from a theme in a number ways. First, themes and concepts appeal to the mind and are often written in passive language. Main movements seek to produce a response or movement in the heart and hands of the listener through active language. Second, a theme expresses itself in thoughts and ideas, but a main movement expresses itself in terms of a purpose. It accomplishes a specific task. Third, a theme or a concept tends to be impersonal. A main movement either explicitly expresses God as the main actor who wants a personal response from his children, or expresses God as the personal recipient of his children's activity.

The main movement is the theme or concept of a text activated, functionalized, and personalized.

A truly moving message has movement. Therefore, it requires active language; it must be **activated**. But, activity without direction and purpose wastes time and energy. Therefore, a moving message needs purpose and direction. It must go somewhere; it must be **functionalized**. But, at this point the message is still technical and abstract, if the preacher fails to apply this truth to the listener's hearts and hands. Therefore, the main thrust of the text must also be **personalized**.

In the main movement, God becomes the main actor who wants a personalized response from his children or God is the main recipient of his people's activities.

The main movement involves three steps: activate, functionalize and personalize. A theme, concept or main thrust must undergo these three steps in order to be transformed into a main movement.

IV. The Main Movement Hits All Birds With The Same Stone

Some books on preaching call the preacher to think at multiple levels, while creating the sermon. For example, O. C. Edwards, in his *Elements in Homiletic* suggests, that preachers write out three statements: your thesis, your purpose, and the response you seek.[4] The approach that I advocate hits these three birds with the same stone by incorporating the thesis, purpose and desired response in one simple statement.

Haddon W. Robinson suggests that the preacher should determine the exegetical idea of the text, take into consideration the audience being addressed and transform it into a homiletical statement. So far so good. That is a good integration of idea and desired result. Then, Robinson seems to suggest that the preacher is to determine the purpose he wishes to accomplish.[5] But, I don't read anywhere about the integration of the purpose into the homiletic idea. To my understanding he does not suggest a rewriting of the homiletic idea in light of the purpose. Rather the purpose remains something that plays a role somewhere in the back of the preacher's mind. If that is the case, the preacher must again write, while thinking at multiple levels.

The main movement incorporates all aspects into one simple statement, so that the thesis, the purpose, and the desired outcome are all expressed as one. If the rest of the sermon is true to its main movement, all of these aspects will unfold naturally in the body of the sermon. Then, there is no need to think at multiple levels. Rather, the aspects are integrated in the mind of the preacher and find their way into the delivered sermon. The main movement approach kills all birds with one stone by incorporating everything into one simple statement. We might call this integrated sermon development.

In order to explain the transformation of a theme into a main movement as concretely as possible, I shall use the story of the wisemen. From Matthew 2:1-12 the story reads as follows.

> *After Jesus was born in Bethlehem in Judea, during the time of King Herod, Magi from the east came to Jerusalem and asked, "Where is the one who has been born king of the Jews? We saw his star in the east and have come to worship him."*
>
> *When King Herod heard this he was disturbed, and all Jerusalem with him. When he had called together all the people's chief priests and teachers of the law, he asked them where the Christ was to be born. "In Bethlehem in Judea," they replied, "for this is what the prophet has written:*

'But you, Bethlehem, in the land of Judah, are by no means least among the rulers of Judah; for out of you will come a ruler who will be the shepherd of my people Israel.' "

Then Herod called the Magi secretly and found out from them the exact time the star had appeared. He sent them to Bethlehem and said, "Go and make a careful search for the child. As soon as you find him, report to me, so that I too may go and worship him."

After they had heard the king, they went on their way, and the star they had seen in the east went ahead of them until it stopped over the place where the child was. When they saw the star, they were overjoyed. On coming to the house, they saw the child with his mother Mary, and they bowed down and worshipped him. Then they opened their treasures and presented him with gifts of gold and incense and myrrh. And having been warned in a dream not to go back to Herod, they returned to their country by another route.

V. Stating The Theme Or Concept

After the preliminary study has been completed, the idea of the text should be stated in one simple statement. Here that idea might read, "The Jews were being put to shame."

A. It is obvious that the statement of the idea must have its basis in the text. The idea should never impose itself on the text, but it should come from the passage itself. Never trample a text with your own "hobby horse." Using all the tools at your disposal, discover the main idea of the text and state it as clearly as you can.

The justification for this theme developed from Matthew 2:1-12 will become clear as you read portions of the sermon in later chapters. However, a preliminary comment is necessary. Matthew is the only gospel writer who records the visit of the magi. He did this partly because his audience was Jewish. The wisemen are particularly embarrassing to the Jews because gentiles from the east came to recognize Jesus as the fulfillment of prophecy before the Jews did. Despite their knowledge of the coming Messiah, the Jews are shamed by Gentiles who have come to worship Jesus. Thus the theme reads, "*The Jews were being put to shame.*"

B. It is important to state this idea as simply as possible. Never use a compound sentence. To put it another way, the statement of the idea must contain no conjunctions.

One evaluator of this book questioned that if the text has conjunctions, shouldn't the theme also have the same conjunctions? If the text has conjunctions, then look for a single theme behind the thoughts joined by the conjunction. State that one theme clearly and then make sub-points from the thoughts joined by the conjunctions. Avoid compound themes at all costs.

Jesus' words in the Sermon on the Mount apply here. "No one can serve two masters. Either he will hate the one and love the other, or he will be devoted to one and despise the other (Matthew 6:24)." Whenever you have two ideas in one theme, you plant the seed for two sermons which may compete with each other. You can't do justice to both because they compete for your attention and muddle the expression of your thoughts. Your allegiance flips back and forth. The result is an extremely complex sermon development that leads to a tornado-type action which sends your listeners spinning.

C. It is important to limit the scope of the statement. As Aho says, "Ordinarily, the more specific the subject, the greater the interest."[6] The more specific your target, the more attention it will draw.

VI. Steps In Transforming A Theme Into A Main Movement

A. ACTIVATE: The first step is to activate the statement by working with the predicate, which is the main verb and its modifiers. In this instance the predicate is: ". . . were being put to shame."

1. The main movement must be a sentence complete with a verb. Some books on sermon outlines and homiletics don't use verbs in the theme, making them extremely weak. Some typical samples are: "Divine Guidance," "In New Pathways," "Lessons From The Triumphal Entry," "Three Crosses at Calvary."[7]

The book from which I took these themes contains approximately 50 themes, but no more than three or four of them have a verb. At best, such statements are titles and not themes. Incomplete sentences with no verbs deaden the heart of your message, you must have a full sentence statement with a lively verb.

2. The main verb in the main movement must be lively and in the active voice.

Other themes I encountered use bland verbs, "It's time to wake up," "We have an extraordinary Lord in our ordinary living," "On being worldly Christians."[8]

These verbs don't inspire movement. If you want a moving message, you need strong active verbs.

I've activated the above quoted themes:

> Divine Guidance, might read God reveals who is in control.
>
> In New Pathways, might read God always leads you down new pathways.
>
> Lessons From The Triumphal Entry, might read God shows (tunes you into) you the nature of his kingdom.
>
> Three Crosses at Calvary, might read God lets you see how the cross of Jesus can affect the way you bear your crosses.
>
> It's time to wake up, might read God Shouts, Wake Up!
>
> We have an extraordinary Lord in our ordinary living, might read God sent an extraordinary Lord in your ordinary lives.

On being worldly Christians, might read God points to the worldliness of your faith.

3. The main verb in the main movement must be in the present tense.

In order to move the listener, the language of the main movement must be in the present tense. In his book, *Design For Preaching*, H. Grady Davis says, "Great preaching is always in the present tense and thus always speaks to the concerns of the day in the thought forms and language of the day."[9]

Looking at our example again, the present theme is as follows:

"*The Jews were being put to shame*"

By activating the predicate, we can change to the present tense and active voice, so it reads:

"*The Jews are put to shame.*"

Although that helps, it obviously leaves much to be desired. So we must turn to the second step.

B. PERSONALIZE: A good way to personalize the statement is to state the idea in terms of "God" and "you."

1. Rewrite the statement and personalize it by using the word "you." Ask yourself, "Where does my audience fit into the main idea?"

For example, the Jews can be paralleled with the New Testament church. By making this change, the statement reads:

"*The church is put to shame.*"

But your congregation is a part of the church, so you can substitute the word "you" in place of "church." "You" can be viewed as plural to refer to the whole congregation. But, it can also be viewed as singular, thus personalizing the statement even more by aiming it at each individual. The statement now reads:

"*You are put to shame.*"

That personalizes the message directly to your audience.

Some think that this approach is too direct and that the preacher should also always include himself in the overall statement. So then the statement reads:

"We are put to shame."

A. K. Straatsma has a chapter on this very issue in the book, *Hoe Vindt U Dat Er Gepreekt Moet Worden*. In translation, he writes, "I remember a comment made to me several years ago by Mrs. Van Hoogstraten-Schoch. She had been in church and had heard me preach. After the service she came to the council room and asked me why I always said, 'you' and not 'we' in my sermon. I considered her insight profound and I determined then to change my ways. Using 'you' gives the impression that you yourself don't need the gospel and that you only stand on the pulpit and not under it. As if, 'I, the preacher, have made it, but now I have to get the rest of you to my level.' "[10] Straatsma's concern is genuine, but I think his difficulty can be dealt with without switching to "we."

By preaching in the first person plural, using "us" and "we" instead of "you," the message becomes less personal for the listener and leaves him with an easy way out. People can easily disregard a point if it is generally addressed to "us" or "we." They tend to apply it to the other guy, to the other part of "us," and not to themselves.

Recently, I spoke to a group of Christian school teachers about my concerns over the lack of an enthusiastic vision for education in the entire Ontario Christian School community. I don't spend a lot of time in Christian schools or with Christian school teachers, so I wanted to be cautious about using the word "you" and applying it directly to them. Instead, I used terms like "we" and "us" and the "broader school community." I consciously did this and I still think, considering the circumstances, it was a good choice. But, I was interested in the kind of response I would receive. The first comment from the audience of Christian school teachers mentioned that it was not they, but rather the constituency that lacked vision and enthusiasm. I left them an out and they took it.

Sinful human beings are naturally that way. If you say something corrective to me in the first person plural, "we," you offer me a way out. With a momentary "flit" of the mind,

I can exclude myself from the audience in question and walk away unaffected. But, if you focus directly on me by using, "you," I cannot so easily disregard it. I must give it more in-depth reflection before I discredit it or take it to heart.

By using "you," your message is personalized. But, then you must be absolutely sure that message does indeed apply to your audience and that you are not "beating a dead horse" or "a straw man." You violate the trust of your congregation and undermine your own integrity if you try to apply to them something that is not true of them.

A moving message speaks in the second person.

As to Straatsma's concern of sounding too authoritarian and holier than thou if you speak in the second person, it can be compensated by explicitly expressing God as the actor in main movements which are directive in style.

2. Personalize the statement by rewriting it in terms of God as the main actor.

"*God puts you to shame.*"

This brings God into a personal relationship with the action. He is the main actor. In every directive scripture passage, God has something authoritative to say to his people. Therefore, it is theologically appropriate that he be portrayed as the main actor in such a movement. Never leave the action of this main movement impersonal. God is actively and authoritatively seeking to arrive at his own purposes in and through you.

When God is expressed as the main actor in directive main movements, people will not be offended by hearing you address them in the second person. They will sense you are speaking for God and not for yourself. It removes the fear of being charged with a holier than thou attitude.

Preachers, however, can get themselves into hot water if they state the main movement according to their own intended purpose. And, they deserve it. By doing so, they draw attention to themselves as the authority and abuse their office. They must speak in terms of God's authority and purpose, not their own.

Not,

"I want to put you to shame."

but rather,

"God puts you to shame."

All of this is very appropriate to scripture. It makes God the main actor and lends his authority to the message.

Now that you have personalized the main movement, it is almost complete.

C. FUNCTIONALIZE: The third step is to rewrite the statement in terms of the purpose of the passage. In other words, functionalize the statement.

You functionalize a statement by using what John E. Baird in *Preparing For Platform and Pulpit* calls "Purpose Indicators." They are the words, how, what, why, when, where and who.[11] Haddon E. Robinson gives the following little poem to help remember them.

I had six faithful friends
They taught me all I know,
Their names are How and What and Why,
When Where and Who.[12]

The purpose of a given text will answer to one of these six questions. Which one it is will become evident through your preliminary study of the text.

In light of the information in the text, ask all six purpose indicators to determine which one the text answers. Most texts will address either "How?" or "Why?" In our example, the text answers the question "How?", with the answer: "by contrasting them with the wisemen."

By incorporating that answer into the statement it now reads:

"God puts you to shame by contrasting you with the wisemen."

Once it is functionalized the main movement is now complete.

These are the three basic steps in transforming a theme into a main movement. The detail of this chapter, however, may have made it difficult for you to keep everything clearly in order. Therefore, to facilitate your use of these steps you may want to use work sheet number one in *The Moving Message Workbook*.

---

1. Paul Lee Tan, *Encyclopedia of 7700 Illustrations*, (Rockville, Maryland: Assurance Publishers, 1979), p, 1079.

2. Haddon W. Robinson, *Biblical Preaching*, (Grand Rapids: Baker Book House, 1980), p. 20.

3. K. Dijk, *De Dienst Der Prediking*, (Kampen, The Netherlands: J. H. Kok, 1955), p. 169-171.

4. O. C. Edwards, Jr., *Elements of Homiletic,* (New York: Pueblo Publishing Company, 1982), p. 72.

5. Haddon W. Robinson, *Biblical Preaching*, p. 116.

6. Gerhard Aho, *The Lively Skeleton: Thematic Approaches and Outlines*, (St. Louis: Concordia Publishing House, 1977), p. 10.

7. Charles R. Wood, *Sermon Outlines for Special Days and Occasions*, (Grand Rapids: Kregal Publications, 1970)

8. Aho, *The Lively Skeleton: Thematic Approaches*, p. 11.

9. H. Grady Davis, *Design For Preaching*, (Philadelphia: Fortress Press, 1958), p. 203.

10. A. K. Straatsma, "Niet Gij, Maar Wij," in *Hoe Vindt U Dat er Gepreekt Moet Worden?*, ed. A. G. Barkey Wolf (Zwolle, The Netherlands: La Riviere & Voorhoeve, 1959), p. 15.

11. John E. Baird, *Preparing For Pulpit and Platform,* (Nashville/New York: Abingdon Press, 1968), p. 58.

12. Robinson, *Biblical Preaching*, p. 67.

Chapter Three

Biblical Grammatical Concerns In Constructing A Main Movement

"Practically every Sunday I leave church feeling downright rotten." That is what I heard when I answered the phone at 9 o'clock one Tuesday morning. A normally subdued lady in my congregation was raging about how she found my preaching oppressive. She had even read a Dutch book on redemptive-historical preaching by S. G. De Graaf and was wondering, "Are your sermons perchance what De Graaf calls 'moralistic?' " Realizing the issue was too large and too emotional for me to handle over the phone, I tried to keep my voice from cracking. I replied, "I will visit you soon to discuss the matter further." I then hung up the phone, broke down and wept.

I had been vigorously applying the methods already described in this book. A few people had already subtly told me that they were beginning to find my preaching irksome. I heard what they were saying, but paid little attention to it, considering it part of the regular criticism that people in public positions can expect. Yet the criticism had lodged in my heart, and the Tuesday morning phone call brought it to the surface.

But after the tears were dried and the emotions were controlled, this incident caused me to re-evaluate my method and it provided an opportunity for growth.

This little trauma brought home the fact I was working under two misconceptions.

First, I thought that in order for preaching to be proclamation it had to be either in the indicative or the imperative mode. So I constructed my main movements in one of these modes. A steady diet of these sermons began to have the effect of a dripping faucet. It wasn't that these sermons were without Christ, as the caller had suggested. Because of the criticism that my sermons were legalistic, I had made a deliberate effort to vividly present Christ as the Mover (see Chapter 7, "The Mover") behind every directive point I made. The accusation of moralism was unfounded. But, the problem remained because I was preaching only in strongly assertive modes. I had been speaking God's Word in only one tone of voice. This worked well for expressing commands, but failed to give expression to God's affections which are best displayed in the exclamatory mode. "God loves you!" for example, can be captured only in the exclamatory mode. By preaching exclusively in imperatives or indicatives, I ended up either distorting or passing by such themes.

In the Bible God speaks in many tones of voice. It is prudent for you to do the same. As a general rule, that is best done by adopting God's tone of voice in the preaching passage. At college and seminary, I studied Greek and Hebrew. One aspect of that study involved identifying the mood of verbs. At that time, I didn't understand why we must engage in this arduous task. Now I do! Identifying the mood of the verb helps you to preach in God's tone of voice.

Second, I operated under the mistaken notion that God is the primary actor in every part of the Bible. That idea worked well in narrative portions of scripture and in the directive statements of the epistles. But, it didn't do justice for the Psalms where God is often not the main player but rather the recipient of human praise and prayer. In the Psalms, man is often the main actor. Because of my one directional view of proclamation, I virtually cut the praise side out of my preaching. For example, the Psalmist says in various places, "Praise the Lord!" If I attempted to set this in a main movement where God is the actor it would read, "God wants you to praise him." That would cut the doxological aspect right out and change the verse to a command, doing violence to the text. In constructing a main movement out of such a text, it would be better to state it, "Praise the Lord!" (The "you" is implied). This makes it an exclamatory expression of man's affections toward God. By so doing, you preserve the direction of the text.

Main movements in which God is the actor I now call, "Divine Movements." Main movements in which God is the recipient I call, "Worship Movements." And each of these can be expressed in five different moods: declarative, directive, exclamatory, interrogative and conditional. You end up with 10 different kinds of main movements.

Divine Movements	**Worship Movements**
Declarative Divine Movement	Declarative Worship Movement
Directive Divine Movement	Directive Worship Movement
Exclamatory Divine Movement	Exclamatory Worship Movement
Interrogative Divine Movement	Interrogative Worship Movement
Conditional Divine Movement	Conditional Worship Movement

Declarative Divine Movement

In this divine movement, God is the main actor and man (you) is the receiver of the action. Also it is in the declarative mode. I call it "declarative" because that better grasps the meaning of the indicative mode. The declarative mode states a fact, it asserts something to be true, it is neither demanding or emotional. It just states the facts.

This type of movement is best suited for biblical narrative, which has God as the main actor and explains certainties about God. Fee and Stuart in their book, *How To Read the Bible For All That It's Worth*, say narratives are God's story. They show what God has done through his people. With a plot and characters, narratives reveal God as the main Actor, the Hero.[1] Since narratives communicate information about God they are best approached by the preaching in the Declarative Divine Movement form.

Robert Alter says that narratives characteristically use an omniscient narrator who is presumed to know what God knows. On occasion, he might remind us of God's assessment and intentions or even what he says to himself about a given incident, person or thing. By this technique, the author communicates certain knowledge about how God deals with his people and creation.[2] To properly preach a narrative, you must take upon yourself the mind of the omniscient narrator and speak a Declarative Divine Movement that dispenses knowledge about God.

God's promises are well expressed in this movement. Therefore, it is appropriate to parts of the Bible that speak in declarative covenantal language: covenants with Noah, Abraham, Moses and the covenant renewals made throughout the history of God's people. A Declarative Divine Movement on the covenant in Genesis 17 might read:

God promises you his covenant blessings. (PI.* is "what?")

This is the basic structure of the Declarative Divine Movement.

God ________ you ____.
(Verb) **(answer to the PI.)**

This could also be stated in discourse.

God says, "I ________ you ________________________________."
(Verb) **(answer to PI.)**

Example: God says, "I promise to bless you."

Miracles and parables are best expressed in Declarative Divine Movement, because they do not stand alone. Frequently, they appear in the context of narratives, in order to reinforce a point being made. Thus, the main movement should be determined by the narrative surrounding the miracle or parable rather than by their internal content.

So, narratives, convenantal statements, parables and miracles are best expressed through a Declarative Divine Movement; a movement that states the facts. But of course the Bible doesn't just give you data to be received for information. When

---

* represents purpose indicator. For a more detailed explanation of this term see Chapter Two.

the Bible faces you with certain particulars about God it intends to create a definite response. A Declarative Divine Movement is meant to cast a response of trust, confidence and assurance. The Bible's facts about God are meant to form a firm foundation for your faith. Such movements should become pillars that support your listener's faith.

Directive Divine Movement

In this movement, God is the main actor, man (you) is the recipient and it is in the imperative mode. I call it the "directive mode" because this best describes the nature of this mode, which expresses a command or a directive.

Aho and Davis say that there are problems in preaching in this mode because it tends to make the tone of the whole sermon moralistic, dogmatic and legalistic.[3] Also, as Davis points out, there is a real temptation to use this mode to accomplish your own ends.[4] These points are important, but some of the difficulty is diminished by making it clear that it is God speaking, not you. It is after all a Directive Divine Movement.

The mode ought to be determined by the text, rather than by any other considerations. If a text is in the directive mode, it is improper to change modes, just to avoid sounding legalistic. There are a lot of other ways to keep from doing so. In particular, you can preach the text in the broader contexts of redemptive history focusing in Christ. This should be done without losing the directive center of the text!

I mentioned, constant preaching in this mode can become like a dripping tap. It can wear your people down. But, if the scripture passage calls for it, don't avoid using this mode for fear of a negative reaction. We live in an individualistic age that dislikes authority. But, that should not prevent preachers from declaring God's claim on their listener's lives. Such a retreat would only further develop the type of culture that existed in Israel at the time of the Judges, when everyone did what was right in their own eyes.

While at seminary, our family lived in inner city Grand Rapids for four years. Like many inner cities, Grand Rapids had its share of crime. We often lived in fear. We were only outdoors to run from the car to house and from the house to the car. Somewhere along the line, decent citizens, out of fear, retreated into the fortresses of their homes. That was a big mistake because they yielded the streets to more unsavory elements.

That can happen in preaching. You can abandon the directive terrain of preaching and retreat to more passive modes. But, if you don't claim this terrain you can be sure other influences will. Therefore, when God speaks in a directive tone, you must speak for him in the same tone of voice. Anything less is an injustice to your congregation, the Word of God and God himself. When you preach in this mode, however, it is of utmost importance to keep the Mover, Jesus Christ, before your audience (see Chapter 7, "The Mover"). Illumine his cross in neon lights. If you don't, your message will indeed "come off" as moralistic. Remind them of the "Declarative Movement" from which the "Directive Movement" arises: Christ went to the cross for you.

The following is the structure of an Directive Divine Movement. The example comes from Hebrews 6:1-3.

God wants you ______________________________ .
(verb) (answer to PI.)

Example: God wants you to forget the kid stuff. (PI is "what?")
This could also be stated in discourse.

God says, "You ought to ______________________________ ."
(verb) (answer to PI.)

God says, "You ought to forget the kid stuff."

While Declarative Divine Movements are good for expressing promises of the covenant, Directive Divine Movements are best for expressing the covenants' demands. Use this mode for preaching commandments or laws. It is also appropriate for the strong directive texts from prophets, many of Jesus' statements in the gospels and admonishments in the epistles. Fee and Stuart call the epistles "task theology." They are not abstract doctrine, but doctrine that is oriented to perform a certain task in the situation.[5] This is best communicated by a Directive Divine Movement. While the Declarative Divine Movement is intended to forge a response of trust and confidence, the Directive Divine Movement creates a rise to definitive action.

Exclamatory Divine Movement

In this divine movement, God is the Actor and man (you) is the recipient. It expresses strong feelings. Aho says with exclamatory preaching the emotional flavor of a sermon is heightened by engaging the listener at a feeling level.[6] It is more than a statement of fact for it provides an emphatic emotional statement of fact.

The Exclamatory Divine Movement captures the affections or displeasures of God and communicates them to your people.

It differs from the declarative by adding emotion. And it always ends in an exclamation mark.

In addition to these characteristics, a recent book on grammar states: "Exclamatives as a formal category of sentence are restricted to the type of exclamatory utterance introduced by "what" and "how."[7] There are only two options of exclamatory movements as shown by the two examples.

What a wonderful love God has for you!

How God must love you!

An Exclamatory Divine Movement has the following structure. The example is based on John 3:16.

What/How ____________ God ______________________ you!
(Purpose Indicator) **(verb)**

Example: What a wondrous love God has for you!
This could also be stated in discourse.

What/How ____________ I ____________________ you!
(Purpose Indicator) **(verb)**

God says, "What wondrous love I have for you!"

This mode is particularly appropriate to the emotional denunciations by many of the prophets, but also to the affectionate expressions of such prophets as Hosea. Many texts in the Gospels and the Epistles of John demand an Exclamatory Divine Movement because they are loving in tone.

The Apocalyptic Literature of Revelation and Ezekiel and Daniel would also be best expressed in this movement. That literature uses exaggerated imagery to communicate the battle between the forces of evil and the kingdom forces. This is an exclamatory means of communication because it expresses facts in exaggerated language and imagery. Since, as Berhard Anderson claims, big symbolism and cryptic language are characteristic of apocalyptic literature,[8] the Exclamatory Divine Movement should be used.

Such movements are generally not intended to create trust and confidence, nor are they necessarily meant to stir people to action. Their purpose is to stir the emotions. If the Exclamatory Divine Movement expresses God's wrath, it arouses a proper fear and awe of God. If it speaks of God's anger against sin, it awakens a genuine feeling of sorrow. If it is an expression of God's love it warms the hearts of your hearers and excites in them affections for God.

Interrogative Divine Movement

This divine movement is expressed as a question. Since there is no big chunk of biblical literature that has this form, it is rarely used. There are, however, individual texts throughout the Bible that are appropriate for the Interrogative Divine Movement. For example, a main movement on Isaiah 5:1-7 (especially verse 4) could be expressed:

What more could God do for you?

It could also be stated in discourse.

God asks, "What more could I do for you?"

A main movement on Matthew 16:13-20 could be expressed:

Who is Jesus to you?

It could also be stated in discourse.

Jesus asks, "Who do you say I am?"

The basic structure is as follows:

_______________ God _______________ you?

(Purpose indicator) (verb)

Stated in discourse:

God asks, "_______________ you _______ I _______ ?"

(purpose indicator) (verb)

Such movements are used in order to instill a reflective response: a response of self-examination. They simulate the contemplative, the meditative and the introspective side of your listeners. In my own church tradition, it is customary to have a "Preparatory Service" the week before the celebration of the Lord's Supper. Such services are meant to begin a week of self-examination, in order that you will be prepared to come to the Lord's Table in the right frame of mind and heart. Preaching on a text that properly yields to the Interrogative Divine Movement would be particularly appropriate for such an occasion.

Conditional Divine Movement

This is a divine movement expressed in the conditional mode. This movement is appropriate for texts that are conditional.

One such text is Matthew 6:33. "But seek first his kingdom and his righteousness, and all these things will be given to you as well." The main movement reads as follows:

God will supply all your needs if you seek his kingdom above all else. (PI. is "how?")

Stated in discourse:

God says, "If you seek my kingdom first,
I will supply all your needs."

According to Davis, there is a danger in preaching in this mode. He says, "The conditional is the mode of the instrumentalist, the pragmatist, and the moral idealist. Its stock in trade is expediency, profit, gain, either temporal or 'spiritual.' (It somehow assumes that selfishness becomes sanctified when its object is 'spiritual.') Its danger is works righteousness, an attempt to bargain with God. The conditional mode misleads people into supposing that they secure God's favor by what they are and what they do."[9]

Indeed, you must guard against this danger. But if you properly present the Mover (see Chapter 7, "The Mover"), it will be clear that you are not encouraging people to do things for pragmatic reasons but for the love of Jesus. In this sense, then, a Conditional Divine Movement answers only to the purpose indicator "how?" rather than "why?". If the purpose indicator is "why?" it would imply expediency. But answering "how" indicates the means by which something is accomplished, rather than the motivation for accomplishing it. For example "seeking first the kingdom" is not why He supplies our needs, it is the means through which He supplies our needs.

This form of movement is appropriate to proverbial statements not only in the Book of Proverbs, but throughout the Bible. Proverbs should not be expressed in the declarative. They do not express facts. Rather they explain the way things usually go in God's kingdom. They express "likelihoods." Bernhard Anderson says they are not legal guarantees from God, but the way things usually go.[10] This uniquely lends itself to Conditional Divine Movements.

Genesis 9:6 illustrates the importance of correctly communicating a text in this mode. "Whoever sheds the blood of man by man shall his blood be shed; . . ."

Traditionally, this text was thought to be a command and therefore put in a directive mode. Recent scholarship, however, speculates that the statement actually has a proverbial form.[11] If, indeed it is a proverb, then it should be preached in the conditional mode. To do so, provides a whole new flavor to the message. It doesn't demand the killing of a murderer, but expresses the likelihood that those who "play rough" are likely to receive the same treatment in return.

If you are preaching on a proverb, it is best communicated in a Conditional Divine Movement.

The structure of such a movement is as follows:

God will ________________ you if ________________ .
(verb) **(answer to PI. "how?")**

Example: God will supply your need if you seek his kingdom above all else.
Stated in discourse:

God says, "If ________________ you ________ I ________ ."
(answer to PI. "how?") **(verb)**

Example: God says, "If you seek first my kingdom I will supply your needs."

All Conditional Divine Movements answer to the PI. "how?"

This type of movement creates a prudent response in your hearers by encouraging them to take well-advised action. In the redemptive context, it shows people how to behave prudently.

In sermons that are conditional, you must allow God to be free. God usually works by the norms found in the Bible's proverbs, but in his sovereignty he is not to be bound by them. Let God be God! He has the right to go contrary to normality if he, in his good judgment, decides that is best for you. And you can be assured that his judgment is good and he knows what is best for you. He sacrificed his own son for you, didn't he? When you preach such sermons, inform your congregation that these proverbs indicate the way things usually go under his divine rule. However, remind them that if things go differently they must not get bitter at God or call his goodness into question. When God departs from the norm he has good reasons, which may not be known to us, but in the light in the cross they are ultimately reasons of compassion and integrity.

Declarative Worship Movement

In this worship movement, the human being (you) is the main actor and God is the recipient of your actions. As well, being in the declarative mode, it states fact. By combining these two ideas, a Declarative Worship Movement confesses and expresses facts about God. This movement best communicates from confessional statements in scripture which are not highly emotional. They just state firmly and clearly certain truths about God. The Psalms contain a number of such statements. For example, Psalm 24 is a confessional psalm. Verse one says, "The earth is the Lord's and everything in it, the world and all who live in it." The Declarative Worship Movements reads as follows:

The world belongs to God because He is God.

(It is implied that "you" are making the confession.)

In discourse, this movement might better be stated:

You confess, "The world belongs to God because He is God."

Declarative Worship Movements take the following form:

______________ God ______________ . (implied confession)
(subject) (verb) **(answer to PI.)**

Stated in discourse:

You confess, " ________________ God ________________ ."
(Subject) (verb) **(answer to PI.)**

In sermons constructed around a Declarative Worship Movement, you draw your congregation as persons and as a whole into a confession about God. The response you want to create is one with God. Together you want God to be praised by your firm confession. It is after all a Worship Movement.

But, such confessional sermons also provide comfort. When you confess great things about your God this will also be consoling for you. Such sermons state facts for God's glory and your comfort.

Those preachers who serve confessional-type churches will find the Declarative Worship Movement helpful for preaching on confessional material. However, there are different ways to preaching on such material.

Some preachers illustrate with a text the doctrinal matter at hand. They then preach a sermon on the text because it is believed to be only proper to preach directly from scripture and not from material derived from it. This approach makes the confession superfluous, and thus negates some of the purpose of having a confession in the first place.

Other pulpiteers also read from the creedal writings and an associated scripture text. But then they preach their sermon on both. By making reference to the creed and scripture, they hope to catch the best of both. This approach divides the focus of your audience and creates a blur in your message. But more importantly, I believe such preaching does violence to the unity of both. If you are going to preach a text, preach a text! If you are going to preach the confession, preach the confession!

My own approach is to preach on the confession itself as if it were my text. As to the argument of preaching only from scripture, I have signed a Form of Subscription which states I believe everything said in the creeds of my denomination truly represents the Word of God. If I believe this, why not preach on the doctrine? And if you, with me, choose to preach from a confession probably the Declarative Worship Movement is the best approach.

In my own denomination, however, preachers are to preach once a Sunday from a confession called the Heidelberg Catechism. This confession is deeply personal and it uses a lot of experiential language. Then, an Exclamatory Worship

Movement best expresses the confession because it states the facts in an emotional manner. This type of movement suits the opening question and answer of the Heidelberg Catechism.

> Q. WHAT IS YOUR ONLY COMFORT IN LIFE AND DEATH?
>
> A. That I am not my own, but belong — body and soul, in life and death — to my faithful Savior Jesus Christ . . .

A Declarative Worship Movement on this would read,

"It is comforting to have Jesus as your Savior."

A Exclamatory Worship Movement on it would read,

"What a comfort it is to have Jesus as your Savior!"

There is more on the Exclamatory Worship Movement later in this chapter.

Because the catechism uses a question and answer format, the issue arises as to whether or not the interrogative movement works here. One might well be justified in doing that.

Confessions have three purposes: for education, for profession before God and fellow believers and a statement of faith over against theological opponents. The purpose for which you use the confessions will determine the mode in which you put it. For education, an Interrogative Divine Movement might be appropriate. Following the format of the catechism you are asked a question and then you are given God's answer based on scripture. For profession of faith before God and His saints, the Exclamatory Worship Movement is the best. For expression of the facts of faith before God and against doctrinal dissension, the most suitable method is a Declarative Worship Movement.

It would seem to me, however, that the most natural mode for confession material is the Declarative Worship Movement.

Directive Worship Movement

In such a movement, the human being (you) is the actor and God is the receiver. The statement is in the directive or command mode. You might say there is no place in scripture for people to legitimately make demands of God. But, look at the verbs in the Lord's Prayer. In the directive mode, they make demands of God. That may not sound correct, but remember God himself commands you to pray for the things you need to serve him. Jesus teaches you this model prayer and through his atonement He has won you the right to demand of God. You can demand of God, as long as you do not insist on personal things. Rather, demand things you need to hallow his name, advance his kingdom, and do his will. Preaching in a Directive Worship Movement is appropriate for the prayers of the Bible. Many of the Psalms are prayers and this movement is particularly suited to them.

You may argue, however, that prayer and preaching are two different types of communication and therefore "prayer-like" movements have no place in a sermon. But, it is very fitting to preach in a prayerful style because you draw your audience into the message by having them share in the prayer. I am moved by a memorable occasion in seminary, when an emeritus minister, Rev. J. Herbert Brink, preached a prayer Psalm by praying an elucidated version of the psalm and including us in it. When you properly preach a prayer, you involve yourself and your listeners in the prayer. And when you communally express to God your needs in this way, he is praised because his children indicate their dependence on him.

Psalm 71 is a prayer demanding salvation from God. The main movement might read as follows: *God grant me salvation.*

(It is implied that "you" are making the prayer)

Stated in discourse it reads as follows: *You pray, "God grant me salvation.*" (PI. is "what"?)

The basic structure of a Directive Worship Movement is as follows:

God______________________________ . (implied prayer)

(verb) (answer to PI.)

Stated in discourse:

You pray, "God ______________________________."
(verb) (answer to PI.)

Exclamatory Worship Movement

This movement directs human praise or doxology towards God. By its emotive character in the exclamatory mode, it is a confession given passionate force. All praise sections of scripture belong in this movement which means extensive use for sermons on the Psalms. Fee and Stuart say that Psalms are intended to appeal to the emotions, to evoke feelings, rather that propositional thinking, and to stimulate a response that goes beyond cognitive understanding of certain facts.[12] Under some circumstances this type of movement may be helpful when preaching on doctrinal material. For an explanation of this, read the material under the heading **Declarative Worship Movement.**

The distinguishing features of this movement are its emotive force, its response to either "how" or "what" and its concluding exclamation mark. It instills a praise response in your hearers. Such a sermon is not so interested in moving your listeners to outward action, as in creating internal praise to God. This may also express itself in a response by the congregation in word or song. Such a movement would read as follows: *Praise the Lord for his goodness*! ("you" is implied, PI is "what?")

It takes on the following structure:

________________ God ______________! (you is implied)
(verb) **(answer to PI.)**

I do not set up this structure in discourse because it cuts at the emotive force. It would sound something like this:

You confess, "Praise the Lord for his goodness!"

With the "you" implied, it preserves the emotive force.

More than half a century ago, there was a trend among some Dutch preachers to end almost every sermon with a doxology, even sermons that were declarative and directive in mode. To do so, removes some of the intended force and direction of the text. But, such an ending is the only way to conclude a Exclamatory Worship Movement Sermon.

Interrogative Worship Movement

This worship movement implies a human (your) action toward God. In the Form of an interrogative, this movement moves from questioning to resolve. Lament or wisdom psalms are best translated into Interrogative Worship Movements because they question God about his goodness and move towards a resolve. At a time of great difficulty or tragedy, you can pick the words from a lament psalm and lead the congregation through all the motions of a soul struggle to the same spiritual resolve as the psalmist. Psalm 44 fits into this type of movement rather well. The psalmist asks the question, "Why have you rejected us?" and then proceeds to explain how they have been rejected. It never reaches a resolve of "why?" but gives the affirmation that God, as in the past, will help. That, in itself, is resolve enough.

The main movement would read as follows: *God, why have you rejected me*? (PI. "why?")
(it is implied that "you" are the questioner)

Stated in discourse: *You ask, "Why has God rejected me*?"

The basic structure of such a main movement is as follows:

God, ______________________________________ ?
(Purpose Indicator) **(verb)**

Stated in discourse:
You ask, "God, ______________________________ ?"
(Purpose indicator) (verb)

As well, the Interrogative Worship Movement is a good way to translate wisdom literature into a preaching style. Wisdom literature deals with the riddles and struggles of life and seeks to provide answers and advice. The interrogative mode fits this type of scripture. As a recent book on grammar states, "Questions are primarily used to seek information on a specific point."[13] Queries provide an opportunity for communicating the wisdom of the Word.

Wisdom literature often calls God's actions into question. But, it ends in affirming God's goodness and sovereignty, which brings people to the praise of God.

At a practical level, this type of sermon preaches well because the interrogative mode completely involves your listeners. Aho says, "Themes in the form of a question not only lend themselves readily to the elucidation of the Gospel, but they are also interesting because they involve the hearer directly."[14]

Conditional Worship Movement

The final type is the Conditional Worship Movement, in which the human being (you) places conditions on God. At first, it would seem that there is no such thing. Seemingly, it is inappropriate for us to place conditions on God in order for him to receive our worship. Further, He has already fulfilled all by creating, redeeming and preserving the world. It would seem, that preaching such a movement, would be at best superfluous. Consider, however, such passages as 1 Corinthians 15:12-19. The text expresses a condition and notice that it is "a contrary to the fact condition." The passage contemplates how terrible it would be if Christ had not been raised. The main mvoement on such a passage should read: *You would be without hope if Jesus had not been raised.*

This "contrary to the fact condition" encourages you to think about how unfortunate you would be if things were other than they are, and how fortunate you are to have things as they are.

This "contrary to the fact" approach, by means of contrast, instills a deeper, richer, sense of awe at the goodness and graciousness of God in the hearts of your listeners. And that is exactly what worship movement is intended to do.

The following is the basic structure of a Conditional Worship Movement:

You would ________________ , if God ______________ .
(verb) **(answer to PI.)**

Expressed in discourse it would read:

You confess, "I would be __________ , if God __________ ."
(verb) **(answer to PI.)**

In conclusion, let me reiterate that the direction and mode of the text ought to determine the direction and mode of the main movement. This does not mean, however, that every sentence in a sermon will have the mode and direction of the main movement. But, if the main movement and the moves (ie. main points, see Chapter 4, "The Moves") are stated in this form, then the sermon will flow to express God's intention and tone of voice.

See Table Number 1 in *The Moving Message Workbook* for a chart on how to translate the various kinds of bibical literature in to an appropriate main movement.

---

1. Gordon D. Fee and Douglas Stuart, *How To Read The Bible For All That It's Worth*, (Grand Rapids: Zondervan Pub. House, 1982), p. 73, 74.
2. Robert Alter, *The Art of Biblical Narrative*, (New York: Basic Books Inc., 1981), p. 157.
3. Gerhard Aho, *The Lively Skeleton: Thematic Approaches and Outlines*, (St. Louis: Concordia Publishing House, 1977), p. 14.
4. H. Grady Davis, *Design For Preaching*, (Philadelphia: Fortress Press, 1958), p. 215.
5. Fee and Stuart, *How To Read The Bible For All That It's Worth*, p. 44.

6. Aho, *The Lively Skeleton: Thematic Approaches and Outlines*, p. 14.

7. Randolph Quirk, Sidney Greenbaum, Geoffrey Leech, Jan Svartvik, *A Comprehensive Grammar of The English Language*, (New York: Longman Inc., 1985), p. 833.

8. Bernhard Anderson, *Out of the Depths*, (Philadelphia: Westminster Press, 1974), p. 206-207.

9. Davis, *Design for Preaching*, p. 215.

10. Anderson, *Out of The Depths*, p. 187.

11. Report 31, "Capital Punishment Study Committee," *Acts of Synod of the Christian Reformed Church in North America,* (Grand Rapids: Board of Publications of the Christian Reformed Church, 1981), p. 462.

12. Fee and Stuart, *How To Read The Bible For All That It's Worth*, p. 170, 171.

13. Quirk, Greenbaum, Leach, Svartvik, *A Comprehensive Grammar of The English Language*, p. 804.

14. Aho, *The Lively Skeleton: Thematic Approaches and Outlines*, p. 14.

Chapter Four

The Moves

John A. Broadus alludes to a well-known warning of Horace when he says, "Preachers . . . at times throw together matters which have as little congruity as the human head, a horse's neck, a body composed of parts from all directions and covered with many kinds of feathers, and the whole ending in a fish tail."[1] A sermon's moves must not suffer from such incongruity. Moves must follow the adage, "Birds of a feather that stick together."

Moves are usually known as the main points of a sermon. And as a main movement differs from a theme, so also moves differ from sermon points in a number of ways. Moves, like the main movement in which they have their origin, must be activated, personalized and functionalized.

By the time you have composed your main movement, the major thoughts of your scripture passage should be in sight. Scribble what you believe to be the main concerns of your text on a piece of paper. Think about how they relate to the main movement. Then select only three to four of these thought units to become the basis for your moves. If you begin with more than three or four thought units, you may be able to subordinate them to one of the major thoughts you have selected.

After a lengthy study of Matthew 2:1-12, I have the following scribbles.

1. It's amazing how three wisemen from the east had a greater expectation of Christ's coming than God's covenant people.

2. It's clear that the story indicates that there is something unhealthy about the relationship between Herod and the chief priests and teachers.

3. It's striking how the chief priests and teachers know the prophesies concerning the Messiah, but they don't go and worship him.

4. The wisemen bow down before the Christ Child with the products of their culture.

With the main movement from the previous chapter spruced up a bit, "God puts you to shame by comparing you with the wisemen," it becomes, "God pokes you in the ribs by comparing you with the wisemen," I have the following moves.

I. God pokes you in the ribs by pointing to your lack of expectation.

II. God pokes you in the ribs by pointing to your worldly accommodations.

III. God pokes you in the ribs by pointing to your immobility.

IV. God pokes you in the ribs by pointing to your narrowness.

To form these moves, I want to alert you of a number of features.

I. The Number Of Moves

A three-point sermon is no joke. I agree with Sweazy when he says, "Much fun is made of the conventional three points, but there are reasons for them. A two-point sermon does not offer enough chance for movement and variety; four may tax the memory."[2] Most of my sermons have three points, the wisemen sermon is an exception. At any rate, there should be no less than two and no more then four points. Three is ideal. I say with Broadus, ". . . three divisions give variety without distracting attention or burdening the memory . . . Three gives the idea of completeness — beginning, middle, end. When racers start in a race, the signal is always "One, Two, Three," neither more nor less. The scripture often uses a threefold repetition as the most emphatic and impressive: Holy, Holy, Holy; ask, seek, knock; etc. Often logical and rhetorical reasons combine to fix three as the number."[3] To have a moving message three moves are best.

II. Activate, Personalize, Functionalize

Like the main movement, the moves must also follow the three basic principles of a moving message: activate, personalize, functionalize.

Each of the moves is a complete sentence with the same present-tense verb in the active voice. Each move is personalized by inserting the words "God" and "you." As well, each of the moves responds and answers to the purpose indicator of the main movement — How?

III. Biblical Grammatical Concerns

As well, the moves of the sermon should be in the same mode and direction as the main movement. This will insure that your sermon hangs together to further communicate the mood and direction of your chosen passage. If your main movement is an Interrogative Worship Movement, your moves should not be Exclamatory Worship Moves, but Interrogative Worship Moves. You may want to depart from this pattern for contrast and emphasis. But on the whole, you should form moves in the mode and direction of the main movement, which is honest to your scriptural text.

IV. Using A Progressive Conversational Sentence

In what I call a progressive conversational sentence, the moves are tied together for a flowing logic through your whole sermon. I gleaned this helpful hint from David Buttrick's book, *Homiletic* in which he writes, "If we think of moves of a sermon as 'topics' to be talked about, joining separate sections will be difficult. As soon as we write out the structure as if it were a conversation, however, logic becomes apparent."[4] He uses the following example of three moves.

1. We are all sinners.

2. We have been forgiven in Jesus Christ.

3. We can live in a new way.

Putting this into a conversational personalized sentence it would read: Be honest: You are a sinner, but you have been forgiven by Christ, so you can now live a new life.

You can notice that the moves now have a logical progression to them which is tremendously helpful in giving a sermon a logical flow.

By using this technique on the moves from Matthew 2:1-12, the conversational sentence would read: God pokes you in the ribs by pointing to your lack of expectation, your worldly accommodations, your immobility, and your narrowness.

This sentence ties the moves together in a logical thought pattern but it lacks a progression, which will not always be possible. The preacher should strive to incorporate such a progression when the scripture passage permits. The Dutch homiletician T. Hoekstra writes, "The divisions of a sermon should be used in such a way that the sermon "walks" . . .[5]

To ensure a flowing logic to your sermon, be sure your moves can be stated in a progressive conversational sentence. When this done, your moves will act as birds of a feather that stick together and not result in the grotesque beast Horace talked about.

The progressive conversational sentence has an added benefit. Homileticians argue whether the major points should be numerically announced in a sermon. Up until the time I read Buttrick's book, I did just that. Although it can help your audience through difficult material and give them a method for packaging the material in their memory, it has disadavantages. Your message becomes a lecture which can detract from the purpose of the sermon. Adams says, "You will not want to announce points ordinarily; they will break the flow of discourse if there is no good reason for announcing them."[6]

Buttrick suggests that a good way of flowing from one point to another and yet keep the points distinct is by using the conjunctions of the conversational sentence.

Buttrick's conversational sentence personalized is again, Be honest: You are a sinner, but you have been forgiven in Christ, so now you can live a new life.

Working from this conversational sentence in cold numerical fashion your sermon would look like this:

1. First of all, you are a sinner.
2. Second, you have been forgiven in Christ.
3. Third, and lastly, now you can live a new life.

Instead, make use of the conjunctions common to conversation.

1. Be honest: You are all sinners.
2. But you have been forgiven in Christ.
3. So now you can live new lives.

Buttrick says, "we reserve categorical thinking for trivia — laundry lists, calendar appointments, cost accounting, and the like. When it comes to making sense out of life, or speaking love, or professing faith, we do not think categorically . . . Most human conversation does not employ laboured transitions but shifts easily, by kinds of logical association, from one idea to another."[7]

Some appropriate conjunctions are "but," "and," "yet," and "so." Another way of flowing from one move to another is to contrast the points by using "On the other hand, . . ." or "That doesn't mean now . . ." (See Table No. 2 in *The Moving Message Workbook* for a more complete list of possible conjunctions.)

If you work with the conjunctions and the transitional phrases in the progressive conversational sentence, numbering the moves will become unnecessary. You will maintain the clarity and distinctiveness of each move, remove some of the academic mood and the distraction of numbering, and ensure that moves flow through the sermon. In applying it to our example, the moves become:

I. God pokes you in the ribs for your lack of expectation.
II. Also for your "chumminess" with the world,
III. And on top of this for your "stuck in the mud religion,"
IV. And your narrow religious perspective.

Summary

In forming the moves make sure there are no more than four and no less than two. Also, there are three basic operations to keep in mind.

1. Activate, personalize, functionalize each of the moves according to the main movement.

2. Put each move in the same mode and direction as the main movement.

3. Tie all the moves together in a progressive conversational sentence.

If you follow these steps, your moves, like birds of feather will stick together. And . . . your sermon will fly.

Worksheet #2 in the *Moving Message Workbook* will also help you work through the procedures described above.

---

1. John A. Broadus, *On the Preparation and Delivery of Sermons*, revised by Vernon L. Stanfield, (San Francisco: Harper & Row, Publishers, 1979), p. 93.
2. George E. Sweazey, *Preaching The Good News*, (Englewood Cliffs, New Jersey: Prentice-Hall, Inc., 1976), p. 82, 83.
3. Broadus, *On the Preparation and Delivery of Sermons*, p. 91.
4. David Buttrick, *Homiletic*, (Philadelphia: Fortress Press, 1987), p. 71.
5. T. Hoekstra, *Gereformeerde Homiletiek*, (Wageningen, The Netherlands: Gebr. Zomer & Keuning's Uitgeversmaatschappij), p. 404.
6. Jay E. Adams, *Preaching With Purpose*, (Grand Rapids: Zondervan Publishing House, 1982), p. 55
7. Buttrick, *Homiletic*,p. 70.

Chapter Five

Developing A Move

Many textbooks of homiletics tell you how to construct a theme, how to find the main divisions of your message and then say, "Go for it!" But, when it comes to developing or amplifying the major divisions these textbooks often leave you hanging. In this chapter, we will deal with how to develop a move.*

The development of a move involves five aspects: an opener, a theological definition, oppositions, experience, and finally a closer.

A. An Opener For The Move

Every move should open up with a short, clear, terse statement of your move. R. C. Sproul suggests a technique of "pause, punch, pause."[1] Introduce a new move by pausing then stating your move in a stout sturdy jab, then pausing again. Follow this by restating your move in two or three short sentences so that it is clearly focused in the mind of your listener and "establishes an initial focus in consciousness."[2] In intimate conversation, the introduction of an idea may be grasped in one sentence. But, repetition is necessary in addressing a group, in order to penetrate the distance between the speaker and the listener and to focus attention.

It's the same for gesturing. In a personal conversation, your motions are low-key. But for a larger audience, they have to be expressive. So also when speaking to a public audience, introducing a new idea requires more than one sentence of normal

*In this area I have received the greatest help from David Buttrick's book, *Homiletic*.

conversation. The concept has to be expressed in three or more sentences to fix the idea in the mind of the listener.

Here is an example from a sermon I preached on Hebrews 6:1-3.

Main Movement: God says to you, "Forget the kid stuff!"

The Moves:

1. God says, "Forget the 'I have tos!' "
2. Similarly, God says, "Forget the 'somedays!' "
3. And God says, "Forget the 'I can'ts' "

The first move opens as follows:

> *God says, "Forget the I have tos!" Kids always say, "Awe, do I have to?" "Do I have to hang up my coat?" "Do I have to put away my boots?" "Do I have to tidy up my room?" "Do I have to do my homework?" Kids always says, "Do I have to?"*

By beginning with a punchy expression of the move followed by a few sentences, you focus the concept for the listener. You must get your move anchored in the minds of your congregation right from the start or their thoughts will just drift off to other things. If that happens, it is your fault for failing to penetrate their consciousnes with the move. And if you lose them on just one of your moves, they will miss the flow and cohesiveness of the entire message.

B. Theological Definition Of The Move

In this portion of the move, the biblical underpinings are presented to the congregation. Provide the necessary background, grammar and word definitions for the listener to convince him that the move is indeed a scriptural message that God wants him to hear, not just words from a preacher's mouth.

That is a basic human right of the pew sitter! He has a right to know how you got this move from the Bible! Lloyd Perry says, "The sermonizer should bear in mind the fact that a thoroughly biblical sermon will find its main points within the passage upon which the preacher is preaching. Since they come directly from Scripture, he should place what we term a scriptural undergirding at the end of each main point."[3]

On the other hand, don't fill your move with more theology than is needed to assure the listener that the move is indeed God's message. I have heard some preachers who just jam pack their sermons with background, word studies and grammatical material. When the congregation leaves church all they can say is, "Boy, our preacher is a smart man!" He didn't communicate the message God wanted them to take home and to their workplace. Such sermons always result in two things: they draw attention to the man and they lack a relation to true life. Sermons should leave the hearers more impressed by God than the preacher. A theological lecture contains too much rubble for the listener to tunnel through to find God. Using more theology than is necessary will bog down your message, rather than keep it moving.

C. Oppositions To The Move

Don't treat your congregation like a bunch of "dummies." Respect the fact that they are going to have some of their own thoughts about what you have to say. They won't empty-headedly accept your interpretation of the Bible and its application because you say it is so. In your message, be prepared to address their objections. Also, recognize that just because you proclaim a certain biblical ideal, that doesn't mean it's going to be easy for them to live it out. Help them to live the move in the midst of oppositions in a hostile world.

A preacher should anticipate where his congregation will object to a move and will encounter opposition if they live it out in society.

Because our sinful nature causes us to object to scriptural norms, a preacher should speak to such oppositions in the sermon. Sometimes, trends in culture cause listeners to oppose or misinterpret a certain point. A preacher should also anticipate and address that. Also, in our society we are confronted with many religious influences which people have incorporated into their own self-styled kind of religion. A preacher who knows his congregation will deal with these religious abnormalities.

This section of the move tries to clear away all misunderstandings and oppositions to the move someone might have.

D. The Move Experienced

The truth and integrity of scripture rests in it being God-breathed. For the Christian, there is no doubt about the Bible's authenticity. You do not have to go to science or your experience to prove the truth of the Bible. You accept it by faith. But, it doesn't become meaningful for you, unless you experience it. In that sense, there is nothing like experience to give you a personal feeling of the truth of scripture. When you can point to the move in action the truth becomes real!

I try to help my congregation experience a move by expressing it in my own experience. I illustrate how the move challenges and corrects me and how I struggle to live by it. As well, I express my successes and blessings from putting the move into action. But, of course, in my 37 years on this planet, I have not experienced everything.

Therefore, to help my congregation, I point to others who show the move at work in their lives.

This is often the most joyous part of the move because you communicate the riches and blessings of the move in action.

E. Close The Move

Every move must have a great closing to wrap up a strong opening. It is important that a move end with a short terse statement. If it does not, the listener will have a hard time discerning where one move ends and another begins. A lack of clarity will smudge the moves. By having separate moves, you isolate certain aspects of the main movement and discuss their particular contribution to the whole message. If you don't end a move strongly, that distinctiveness is obscured and the congregation loses the solid handles they need for listening. They are given an opportunity to let their minds wonder.

As well, it is important, that the closing statement not be a compound sentence. A compound sentence creates a divided focus and smudged movement.

I often use a series of short terse sentences in rapid succession concluded with Sproul's "pause, punch, pause" method. I end up with a punch, punch, pause, punch, pause. To see these five aspects of a move in action, I return to the Hebrews 6 example.

Main Movement: God says to you, "Forget the kid stuff!"

The Moves:

1. God says, "Forget the 'I have tos!' "
2. Similarly, God says, "Forget the 'somedays!' "
3. And God says, "Forget the 'I can'ts!' "

The Development Of The First Move:

Opener

God says, "Forget the I have tos!" Kids always say, "Awe, do I have to?" "Do I have to hang up my coat?" "Do I have to put away my boots?" "Do I have to tidy up my room?" "Do I have to do my homework?" Kids always says, "Do I have to?"

Theology

Well, where is this kid's stuff in the text?

Our text says in chapter 6:1, 2: "Therefore, let us leave the elementary teachings about Christ and go on to maturity, not laying again the foundation of repentance from acts that lead to death, and faith in God, instruction about baptisms, the laying on of hands, the resurrection of the dead, and eternal judgment."

Does that sound like kid's stuff to you? It sounds like some pretty solid stuff to me: repentance, faith, baptism, laying on of hands, the resurrection of the dead, and eternal judgment.

That sounds like solid stuff to me!

What you have to realize, as most commentators point out, is that none of this is specifically Christian. It's also Judaism, and it is Judaism that these hearers are in danger of falling back into.

The Jews believed repentance was necessary. They had faith in God to control their life and to send the Messiah. The Jews had baptisms called ceremonial abolutions which were ceremonial washings they went through according to the law (Hebrews 9:10). They had the laying on of hands for ordination to office. The Jews believed in the resurrection the dead. Pharisees and Saducees were always hassling over this doctrine. And certainly the Jews also believed in eternal judgment.

These are not necessarily teachings of Christ, they are simply teachings upon which the doctrine of Christ is built.

So the text is saying, "Forget the kid's stuff of Judaism, and get on with the teachings of Christ."

Opposition

You might say, "Well, I'm not a Jew, so why are you telling me about this?"

Hear me out and see whether you are a Jew or not?

The first thing that shows the Jewish faith is kid's stuff is its legalism.

The Jewish faith is a religion of "have tos." You have to do this and you have to do that.

That is in our text as well. You have to repent. You have to have faith. You have to have abolutions. You have to have laying on of hands.

Legalism is, "Have tos, have tos, have tos." That is kid's stuff.

And they even tried to put a number on the number of things they had to do and number of things they can't do. That is kid's stuff.

Have tos, have tos, have tos and can't dos, can't dos, can't dos, and if you do God's going to spank you.

Now tell me whether you're Jewish or not?

How much of your Christian life is saying, "I have to do this and I have to that? And I can't do this and I can do that?"

And you may even ask, "Well, isn't that what it is to be a Christian?"

God says, "No, forget that kid's stuff."

God says to you, "Grow up!"

Experience

And you say, "How?"

I'm glad you asked.

How can Christians be more grown up, and get beyond the have tos and can'ts?

Well, in what precedes our text, the author has just talked about the great high priest after the order of Melchizedek.

Just read with me, again for a moment, chapter 5:7-11,

> "During the days of Jesus' life on this earth, he offered up prayers and petitions with loud cries and tears to the one who could save him from death, and he was heard because of his reverent submission. Although he was a son, he learned obedience from what he suffered, and once made perfect, he became of the source of eternal salvation for all who obey him and designated by God to be high priest in the order of Melchizedek."

The author has pointed you to the one who suffered all through his life, especially on the cross for your sins, so that you can have eternal salvation.

When you see someone who has suffered, so much for you then you don't ask, "Now do I have to do this for him? Does that mean because of him, I can't do this anymore?"

When you see what he has done for you, you grow up and drop the "have tos" and "can'ts." That is kid's stuff. When you come to grips with what Jesus has done on the cross for you, begin to say, "I want to do this for him," and ask, "What can I do for him?"

That is mature Christian living.

Brothers and sisters how much are you still caught up in this kid stuff? How much of your Christian living is still just a bunch of have tos and can'ts?

Look at the great high priest on the cross again. Dare to look at His nail pierced hands and feet. Dare to admit that His death was for you. Then your childish vocabulary of "having to" will change into "Wanting to."

"Awe do I have to . . .?" That is childish, legalistic language. "For Jesus sake I want to . . .," that is mature Christian language.

If that is not your language, then you better visit the cross again . . . as we will be doing, during this Lenten season.

Ask not, "Do I have to go to church?" That is childish. If you have been to the cross you will say, "I want to go to church."

Ask not, "Do I have to remain married to the same person for the rest of my life." That is childish. If you have been to the cross you will say, "I want to remain married to the same person for the rest of my life."

Closer

Brothers and sisters examine your language. Are you still talking the language of a spiritual three-year-old? Forget that kid's stuff. Start talking like someone who has been to the cross.

This is the method of move development that I use most often. But, it may be good to change the order of theology, oppositions, and experience from move to move for the sake of variety in the sermon.

Hopefully, this method of move development should provide you with ways to guide you in the relatively unexplored field of move development.

Worksheet #3 in *The Moving Message Workbook* will help you work with this methods of move development.

---

1. R. C. Sproul, "Drama in Speaking," *How to Grow Your Church*, (Orlando, Florida: Ligonier Ministries, 1986), video.

2. David Buttrick, *Homiletic*, (Philadelphia: Fortress Press, 1987), p. 38.

3. Lloyd M. Perry, *Biblical Preaching for Today's World*, (Chicago: Moody Press, 1973), p. 54.

Chapter Six

Biblical Literary Concerns In Shaping The Form Or Style Of The Moving Message

Recently, there has been a growing interest in the interpretation of the Bible from a literary point of view. Pastors as well as scholars are taken with this important concern. To say that the Bible is literature is not to question the historicity or factual truth of scriptures, but it simply acknowledges that the authors wrote down God's Word in a specific way to communicate a specific message. Knowing their methods of communicating certainly helps to understand the text.

This approach has recently sparked interest among preachers not only as a means to understand the text, but also as a means for determining the form a sermon should take. Faithfulness to scripture means not only getting the right meaning, but also communicating it in a style that best represents the mood of the entire text.

Chapter two discussed the forming of a main movement. And, Chapter Three dealt with grammatical concerns in constructing a main movement which best represents the mood and direction of text. But, as Sidney Greidanus points out, "Proper formulation of the theme by itself, therefore, is not sufficient to keep the sermon on the right track; one must also consider the form in which the message will be presented."[1] The form of a sermon is the way the moves of a sermon flow and progress into or from the main movement. Greidanus argues that the form of the sermon should respect the form of the text.[2] I appreciate this new emphasis in preaching because it shows respect for scripture. Not only does it honor the Holy Spirit inspired meaning of scripture, but it shows high esteem for the Spirit's choice of literary form and style. This effort definitely gives a more holistic picture of God's message.

In this chapter, we look at shaping the flow and progression of the moves of a sermon and the influence that various forms and styles of biblical literature have on this process.

Basically, there are two types of sermon form: deductive and inductive (see Figure 1).

In the deductive form, the main movement of the sermon is revealed in the introduction, from which the moves then flow. In other terms, a deductive sermon first states the general point of the whole message (the main movement) and then develops the particulars (the moves).

The deductive sermon is the most direct way to communicate your message to those sitting in the pews. But, I know there are those, including my own wife (who has a degree in English literature), who find it less appealing than some other forms. Its simplicity can make it monotonous and its directness can make it less stimulating to the imagination. In my experience, a more educated congregation is less likely to find a deductive sermon appealing. Because a constant diet of these sermons can become monotonous and sterile for even the most ordinary of people, I am attempting to vary them with inductive sermons.

In the inductive form, the moves flow into the main movement. With this method the particulars proceed into the general over all point of your message. The introduction only sets out the first move rather than the whole main movement. The move is then followed by linked moves, until the main movement emerges in the conclusion. I have found the constructing of inductive sermons difficult. But I have found a comment made at a workshop by Rev. Wilbert M. Van Dyk, Professor of Homiletics at Calvin Theological Seminary, helpful: "If you want to form an inductive message take your deductive sermon and turn it up side down." Take the last move of your deductive sermon and introduce it first and then proceed through the other moves. Conclude with some form of what was formerly your introduction.

In an inductive sermon, a listener participtes in the discovery of the truth. The listener accompanies you through the specifics to discover the main point of the scripture passage. Ralph L. Lewis provides further benefits of this sermon form in his book *Inductive Preaching* (Helping People Listen). The second appendix to that book lists all the fabulous characteristics of the inductive method. He has three pages of them, including the following comments on inductive preaching, "Accents human experience and learning from experience." "Assumes positive sharing posture — not defensive negative stance."[3] I find this all a bit too fantastic, for the deductive need not be void of such characteristics either. But, I can see that this sermon form has its time and place, especially with a well-educated congregation. Haddon W. Robinson also suggests an inductive sermon for a hostile audience.[4] That is understandable. If you know your audience is hostile to your subject, then stating the main movement at the start may turn them off to your sermon. But, if you build up to it by linking one move to another, they may be more receptive.

It is not my intention here to claim one form is better than another because they both have their strengths and weaknesses. While the deductive approach can sound dogmatic, the inductive method can give the listeners the impression they are the makers of truth. Depending on how they are handled, both methods can have unsavory side effects. On the positive side, the deductive approach is simple, while the inductive approach stimulates the imagination.

One could argue that a sermon can be deductive/inductive or inductive/deductive (see Figure #1). But this is rare. Either the sermon is more of one than the other. Therefore, I shall limit the discussion to these two basic forms.

However, as already indicated, the more important consideration in determining your sermon form should be the scripture passage itself, and not the nature of your audience, or the desire to make your message more palatable.

Various types of biblical literature are usually presented in a form that is unique to themselves. Whereas the narrative parts of scripture are normally inductive, the didactic parts are usually deductive in form. And the aesthetic or more artistic parts of scripture (such as the Psalms and the apocalyptic literature of some of the prophets and the book of Revelation) reveal the use of both the inductive and deductive forms.

Basically, I work with four styles of sermon: Inductive Narrative, Deductive Didactic, Inductive Aesthetic and Deductive Aesthetic.

Inductive Narrative Style

In preaching narrative passages, the sermon should follow the storyline of the text. This is not a concession to loose sermon structure because such sermons should still have distinct moves which come from the plot of the text and end with a clear statement of the main movement. Notice the words "distinct" and "clear." Sometimes I hear narrative sermons that still leave the whole point of the story unclear for the purpose of some artistic effect. But the whole point of preaching a sermon is to clarify what the story is saying to your congregation! If the sermon leaves the point of the story unclear, you have done your congregation a tremendous disservice.

Stories are usually told in an inductive fashion. From the introduction, the plot-line evolves revealing more and more story until it is completed in the climax and conclusion. Thus, sermons on narrative passages are best done in the inductive form. Indeed, in my experience I have only been frustrated by trying to place a narrative passage in the deductive form. Somehow the material doesn't yield itself to deductive thought and development. And in such sermons you usually end up giving the essence of the story in the first move and the subsequent moves tend to be redundant, lacking in interest.

Truths are written into stories, so that they produce an emotional impact for the people. Plain, theoretical or intellectual teaching often fails to do this. That emotional effect is largely created by the inductive form. A deductive sermon for such a story loses the emotive punch or "wow-effect," as some call it.

Following through on this sort of thinking we must conclude that the sermon on Matthew 2:1-12 is not in its best possible style. The example is a narrative portion of scripture in a deductive rather than an inductive style. This sermon, following the plot-line, should reveal the main movement at the end rather than the beginning in order to be more true to the text.

At present the deductive outline goes as follows.

Introduction: (introduces the main movement)

God pokes you in the ribs.

Moves:

1. For your lack of expectation.
2. Also, for your "chumminess" with the world,
3. And on top of this for your "stuck in the mud religion."
4. and your narrow religious perspective.

Conclusion: (restates the main movement and summarizes the moves.)

Such an approach hits your audience right between the eyes. It is almost too direct! This may be the very reason why the Lord has communicated the message in story in the first place. So the message sneaks its way into your listeners rather than hits them with it. In order to do the same for our sample sermon, it may be necessary to turn it into an inductive form. To accomplish this effectively, it is necessary to use the method of the Prophet Nathan when he told David the "lamb stealing story" in 2 Samuel 12. Nathan refrains from telling David who the story is about until the end. You may have to do the same with a sermon on the wisemen. Leave the second person pronoun out of the moves and only reveal the "you" in the expression of the main movement in the conclusion. Following the plot-line the outline would look something as follows,

Introduction: (introduces only the first move)

Moves:

1. The wisemen have an eager expectation for the coming of Christ,

2. which is not easily compromised with the world,
3. that is accompanied by an active faith,
4. and reveals itself in a broad religious perspective.

Conclusion: (reveals the main movement)

What a contrast to the Jews. You are the Jews!

God pokes you in the ribs.

This form better catches the narrative intention of the text.

In writing an inductive narrative sermon, you should use a limited number of illustrations. The narrative itself is an illustration of sorts so any further illustrations tend to compete with the story and the natural mood of the passage. They tend to blur the focus of the message. Parables and miracles, which are usually couched in a narrative, are also best communicated in the inductive narrative style.

Deductive Didactic Style

The deductive didactic method works best with the Epistles and the proverbial style of wisdom literature. Some wisdom literature (such as Job) is in the narrative form, while, at other times, it is in an aesthetic form (as with the Psalms), But, the proverbial form of wisdom literature (eg. in Proverbs and Ecclesiastes) is best conveyed in this style. This literature, along with the didactic type of literature in the Epistles, is meant to teach or give instruction on how to live as God's people.

Fee and Stuart say that the epistles contain lengthy arguments divided into subdivisions.[5] These arguments are for teaching and often set in a deductive form. In these instances, it is better to use a deductive teaching style.

For the wisdom literature of Proverbs and Ecclesiastes, Ryken says it consists of concise, compacted statements of biblical truth.[6] As opposed to the more theoretical didactic material of the Epistles, these teachings are more practical, lending themselves to a deductive approach.[7]

A good illustration of this style is the sermon I preached titled, "Forget The Kid Stuff." It's based on Hebrews 6:1-3.

Introduction: (introduces the main movement)

God says to you, "Forget the kid stuff."

Moves:

1. Forget the "I have tos."
2. as well as "someday's,"
3. and the "I can'ts."

Conclusion: (restatement of the main movement and a summary of the moves)

In this style of preaching it is good to draw on plenty of illustrative material to back up the moves. The teachings of the Epistles, Proverbs and Ecclesiastes usually have an illustrative partner in a biblical narrative. You may find it helpful to draw on that. R. C. Sproul suggests one such combination, is using the story of the sacrifice of Isaac in Genesis 22 as an illustration of the emotion involved John 3:16, "For God so loved the world that he gave his one and only son, that whoever believes in him shall not perish but have eternal life."[8]

Inductive Didactic Style

Inductive and didactic are two terms that practically contradict each other. For teaching, you want things to be clear and concrete as well as more directive than suggestive. On the other hand, the inductive form tends to be just the opposite; and less concrete. For that reason I do not officially list this form as one of the four possible preaching styles. But, as some have suggested, there is usually a story behind every teaching or argument in the Epistles. If you use that story as a basis for an inductive sermon, it may be effective.[9] But, what is lost is the concrete nature of the teaching.

There are also stories behind the practical teachings of the Proverbs and Ecclesiastes. Building inductive sermons on the story behind the text is also effective. In fact, the book of Job does this when it places wisdom teaching in a narrative form. But, when you see how the book of Job has become a victim of confusion and often contradictory interpretations, you understand why a preacher may opt for a more didactic approach. When preaching wisdom literature and Epistles, you will want the clarity of a deductive didactic approach.

Inductive and Deductive Aesthetic Style

An aesthetic style uses the more artistic forms of communication such as metaphor, imagery, and symbolism. Much of this literature is found in the Psalms, the Prophets, and the book of Revelation. You should grab on to these wonderful images to develop them in your message. Whether you use these passages inductively or deductively will be largely determined by the form of the text. For example, the imagery of Ezekiel 1 or Revelation 4 lends itself to an inductive development because their authors keep building toward the whole picture.

Hebrew poetry (Psalms) is usually composed of three parts: first, a statement of the theme or presentation of the stimulus; second, the development of the thought or emotions of the author on the subject; and finally, a resolution of the thought or emotion.[10] If you have a Psalm that begins with a theme then, of course, that implies a deductive development. If it starts with some kind of stimulus and ends in a resolution, then that suggests an inductive form.

But, the key to grasping the mood of this type of literature is to work with its imagery. It almost goes without saying that then you will not use a lot of outside illustrative material. You will confine yourself to developing the imagery of the text. The following is an Inductive Aesthetic outline of a sermon on Ezekiel 1.

Introduction: (introduces only the first move)

Moves:

1. God sends you out to bring the whole world back to a recognition of his rule (Creatures, vs. 5-10).
2. God is present with you in your struggles for his kingdom (Wheels, vs. 15-18).
3. God empowers you by the sunshine of his Son (the one above the platform, vs. 22, 26-28).

Conclusion:
Main Movement: God has the whir and the blur of your lives under his control.
A Deductive Aesthetic outline of Psalm 122 reads as follows:
Introduction: (introduces the main movement)
How great it is to go to church! (''you'' implied)
Moves:
1. Because it is the place where you get your head together,
2. Plus your heart together,
3. And your act together.
Conclusion: (restates the main movement and summarizes the moves)

Conclusion

Preaching is a literary form all of its own. When you preach you are not telling a story or reciting poetry, nor even teaching a lesson. You are proclaiming God's Word. But, your preaching can be nuanced according the unique literary form of your text. Although the lines of differentiation are not all that distinct, hopefully the material of this chapter will connect your preaching and the text. Perhaps this material will help you communicate God's purpose to your congregation in a more holistic fashion, so that not only the meaning and grammar, but also the arrangement of the sermon will harmonize with God's intention. When God communicates through a story, you should be able to maintain some of the story's emotive character. When God speaks through aesthetic means, you should be able to preserve some of the poetic or symbolic character. When God speaks in direct teaching, you should be able to give instruction with some of the same clarity and concreteness. See Table #4 in *The Moving Message Workbook*.

---

1. Sidney Greidanus, *The Modern Preacher and The Ancient Text*, (Grand Rapids: William B. Eerdmans Publishing Company, 1988), p. 141.

2. Ibid., p. 20.

3. Ralph L. Lewis with Gregg Lewis, *Inductive Preaching*, (Westchester, Illinois: Crossway Books, 1983), p. 194.

4. Haddon W. Robinson, *Biblical Preaching*, (Grand Rapids: Baker Book House, 1980), p. 125-127.

5. Gordon D. Fee and Douglas Stuart, *How To Read The Bible for All That It's Worth*, (Grand Rapids: Zondervan Publishing House, 1982), p. 46.

6. Leland Ryken, *Literature of The Bible*, (Grand Rapids: Zondervan Publishing House, 1974), p. 243.

7. Gleason L. Archer Jr., *Survey of Old Testament Introduction*, (Chicago: Moody Press, 1977), p. 437.

8. R. C. Sproul, "Drama In Speaking," *How To Grow Your Church*, (Orlando, Florida: Ligonier Ministries, 1986). Video.

9. Greidanus, p. 335.

10. Ryken, p. 124.

Chapter Seven

The Mover

The story has often been told of a brass plate mounted on an antique oak pulpit which is visible only to the preacher. The plate's engraving quotes the words of John 12:21, "Sir, we would like to see Jesus."

Although these words are taken out of context, the story does make an important point. In every sermon, your listeners should meet Jesus as the Mover behind the action of your sermon. Jesus must be the Mover in the moving message. He must be the Power behind the drive train of your whole sermon.

Many books on homiletics omit this important matter when it comes to sermon construction. A few books have a bit to say about the importance of Christ-centered sermons. But, when it comes to the practical "how-to," we are left with very little to go on.

The practical point is that Christ fits into your message as The Mover. In every Scripture passage, He is either moving you toward Himself or moving you to some action on his behalf. This should come to full expression in the sermon. Jay Adams eludes to how Paul's preaching centered on Christ as the Mover: "So, when you preach about giving, preach it in the light of Christ's matchless gift as Paul did (2 Corinthians 9:15). When you preach about a husband's love for his wife, preach it in the light of the love of the cross (Ephesians 5:25). When you preach about work, preach it as service to Christ (Colossians 3)."[1] In each instance, Christ is the Mover behind the action of giving, loving and working. If you preach in this manner, no one can accuse you of moralism.

There are two aspects involved in placing Christ before your congregation. First, where do you find him in your text and second, where do you place him in your sermon?

I. Where do we find The Mover

Mark Bolhofner in his book *Evangelistic Preaching In The Local Church* has some helpful suggestions to find Christ in any given text. Christ flows from every text, all you have to do is look for Him. You can find Him in the words and the grammar, the context, the typology and the history of redemption and the theology.[2]

A. In The Words And Grammar

Bolhofner uses the following text. "Therefore, as God's chosen people, holy and dearly loved, clothe yourselves with compassion, kindness, humility, gentleness, and patience . . ." (Colossians 3:12) Such powerful words as "chosen," "holy" and "dearly loved," he says, are open doors to express the good news.[3] The "chosen" are the chosen in Christ. This gives you the opportunity to preach him. You are made "holy" only through Christ which again grants another open opportunity to preach Christ. "Dearly loved" makes you ask, "Loved by whom?" You are loved by God, of course. "How do I know God loves me?" The cross of Jesus Christ is proof that God loves you. These words become opportunities to preach Christ as the Mover who moves us to compassion, kindness, humility.

B. In The Context

The sample sermon on Hebrews 6:1-3 illustrates how Christ can be found in the passage's context. The text is surrounded with references to the great high priest in the order of Melchizedek. The sacrifice of this great High Priest that moves us to forget the kid stuff and go on to maturity. In this instance, you find Christ, the Mover, in the context.

In the story of the wisemen, Christ is found in the center of the text. He is The Babe in Bethlehem who draws the wisemen to worhsip him. So also if you truly know Him as Messiah, the King of the Jews, you will be drawn to worship him. If you truly know Him as your Savior, you will eagerly expect his return, embrace Him only, and make no accommodations with the world. You will worship him with the whole of your life. Again, Jesus is the Mover.

C. In The Typology And The History Of Redemption

Using typology involves finding types or symbols of Jesus and His reconciling work in a specific text. This approach is often used for Genesis 22. As Abraham is offering Isaac, a ram is found in the thicket and used as a substitute. The ram is often used as a symbol of the (substitutionary) atonement of Christ. Although this is meaningful in many instances, I am not always impressed by typological approaches that bring Jesus into the text. In my own theological tradition, I have seen it abused to the point where everyone from Joseph to David is seen as a type of Christ. This practice imports a lot of baggage into the text that neither the secondary authors nor the primary author, the Holy Spirit, ever intended. The Bible authors in the Old and New Testaments do, of course, use typology in their writings. The chosen people of Israel in the Old Testament are a type of the church in the New Testament. But, it becomes pointless when every self-denying act of an Old Testament hero is paralleled to Christ and every drop of blood shed by a Bible character is paralleled with the atonement. In many instances, it is preferable to see Christ as the Mover who worked in these men, rather than to draw a bland, ineffective parallel.

Christ can also be seen through the historical redemptive method. Again, if used properly, it is very helpful. However this method can become stagnated. In my tradition, Christocentricity, for some preachers, means nothing more than connecting every text directly to the incarnation or the cross, as Sidney Greidanus points out.[4] This kind of message may prove an important theological point, but it fails to provide anything truly edifying for the hearer. That is not to deny the historical redemptive approach to interpreting scripture. But, true preaching doesn't preach the method, it preaches the fruits of the method in an edifying way. Whether Old or New Testament, this method shows that every text, in its own time in history, is related to the Cross. When you find how Christ moves a given text, you will be one step away from discovering how the text is intended to move people today.

With this method, Christ is "retro-actively" present in every Old Testament text and "post-actively" present in every New Testament text. Present from eternity to eternity, he is even active in parts of Scripture that pre-date and post-date his incarnation. The benefits of his incarnation are as active in Old Testament as they are in New Testament. In this way, you see Him not so much as a type of Joseph or David but as the Mover in the lives of Joseph and David. Greidanus writes, *This conception of Christ as the eternal Logos, actively at work throughout history, removes the props from under the traditional insistence that every sermon somehow points to Christ Incarnate, in order to be Christocentric. It bursts the confining mold which has caused so many aberrations throughout the history of preaching; it creates more room for the text itself to speak. The preacher is no longer required to land with an acrobatic leap at Golgatha, in order to make the text and the sermon Christocentric, for Christ is already present at that point of redemptive history which the text relates.*[5]

Christ is the main actor and motivator in every text of the Bible.

D. In The Theology

Bolhofner says, "Some portions of Scripture demand to be preached in light of the context of the Bible as a whole and its doctrine. The book of Proverbs is a classic example."[6] Preaching from Proverbs in isolation from the rest of the Bible would lead to gross moralism. The Proverbs have to be placed in their total Biblical-theological context, so that Christ is seen as the Mover behind these great truths. They only make sense in the context of God's grace through Christ as the Mover.

One way or another, if you look for Christ in your Scripture portion you will find Him: in the words, the context, typology, history of redemption, or in the theology behind it. The main problem is that many preachers do not look for him. They just look at a text as a spring board to say something profound. But, without finding Him and putting Him in your message, you will have a message without The Mover and it will go nowhere. And that is hardly profound.

II. Where do you put The Mover?

After you have found Christ in your scripture text, where do you put him in your message? For advice, I again refer to Mark Bolhofner who says, "Once you have found Christ and the Gospel in a text aimed chiefly at challenging believers to grow, you are then able to articulate the good news in the course of your sermon as you deal with that portion of the passage. Doing this you will find that you will be preaching the gospel in your introduction one week, in the transition from the introduction to the main body of the sermon another week, in one of your main points another week, and yes, quite possibly in your conclusion in one of the weeks that follow. The Gospel will flow naturally, powerfully. It will be a vital part of the whole message, the foundation of all you have to say. You will be preaching!"[7]

I wholeheartedly agree with his advice. But, I would not be as cavalier to leave the placement of the Mover in the sermon to the natural course of things, as Bolhofner seems to suggest. I prefer a more deliberate approach which provides a full-bodied articulation of the gospel: in the introduction, one of the moves, or the conclusion.

Every sermon should somehow make a reference to its evangelical stance early in the message. A full expression of the gospel may be left for the conclusion, but an early short reference should be made. This practice will keep your message from being taken as mere moralism and it will put the power of the cross behind the response you call for. I also suggest that the strongest calls to action in your message be juxtaposed with a direct reference to the cross as the ultimate motivator. That will prevent the ever-present danger of moralism; the sin that so easily clings to all preachers.

Many speakers and preachers try to motivate their audience without a Mover, or they try to move the audience themselves. Without a mover, you can't move your listeners to do anything. And if you try to move them yourself, by your own charisma, the church will only move as long as you are there — and for all the wrong reasons. But, if Jesus Christ is the Mover in your message, you have the ultimate power to move people. People will possess power that will continue to move them along after you have left. This kind of preaching in the early church allows you to be beneficiaries of the gospel today, even though you know relatively few of its preachers. Not a dramatic preacher, but Jesus Christ is the real Mover of the church throughout the centuries.

If this absence of a Mover existed only in the sermons of ministerial candidates, there would probably be no reason for concern. But, I am discouraged by sermons and addresses by today's popular teachers and preachers. In the church I serve we recently viewed a film series by James Dobson titled, *Turn Your Heart Toward Home*, and another by Gary Smalley, *Love Is A Decision*. These excellent teachers have a lot of good practical advice for marriages and families, but their messages were void of The Mover. They give us all kinds of "neat" advice, but that advice is of no value to the Christian or non-Christian unless one is motivated to use it. There is no direct reference to The Mover whose cross moves us to put such good advice into action. Human beings are not animals to program to behave the way we want. They react according to the condition of their hearts. And if their hearts have not been touched by the love of Jesus, good advice is not going to do anything to them.

While in California for study, I went to Los Angeles to hear a sermon by John MacAarther Jr. This gifted man spoke of some practical ways in which we can become more and more what we are, the church. But, in his sermon, I never heard the words "cross" or "Jesus Christ." Such teaching, no matter how exegetically correct will not move the church of God. On the following weekend I went to San Diego to hear a sermon on resolving conflict by the Baptist preacher Daniel Baumann, who has written a substantive book on preaching. In discussion with a fellow student afterward, we concluded that the cross and the atonement of Christ had only been implied and not been explicitly articulated in the sermon. Understand me correctly, I have no doubts about the faith or gifts of these brothers. If it were the Christian thing to do, I would envy their commitment and talent. But sirs, I wish to see Jesus.

If you are going to preach a moving message that will change people, you must make explicit reference to The Mover, Jesus Christ and his cross. Don't assume or merely implicate in your message. Be deliberate in making sure that he is there!

---

1. Jay E. Adams, *Preaching With Purpose*, (Grand Rapids: Zondervan Publishing House, 1982), p. 152.
2. Mark O. Bolhofner, *Evangelistic Preaching in The Local Church*, (Unpublished manuscript), p. 4.
3. Ibid.
4. Sidney Greidanus, *Sola Scriptura*, (Toronto: Wedge Publishing Foundation, 1970), p. 144, 145.
5. Ibid, p. 145.
6. Bolhofner, p. 6.
7. Ibid, p. 6, 7.

Chapter Eight

The Moving Start

I am seven years younger than my nearest sibling. As a result, I spent a lot of time entertaining myself around our farm home in South Central Ontario. Many times I pretended that I was a major league pitcher trying to strike out some of the greatest batters of the day. I would pick a small rectangle of approximately four by eight inches located about three and half feet up the outside wall of our old insulbrick home, and I'd throw a tennis ball to hit the spot. If I managed to hit it, it was a strike. If I missed, it was a ball. I was getting so good at it I could, on occasion, pitch a perfect game.

One of the most dramatic parts of the whole charade was imitating the wind-ups of my TV heroes. Standing still for a few moments to concentrate on the target, I would pull up my left leg to about nose level, stretch my right arm far back behind my shoulder and then dramatically "whip" the ball at the insulbrick rectangle.

In this childhood memory, I see parallels between the wind-up and the introduction of a sermon. They involve a similar structure, principles and techniques.

I. The Structure Of A Moving Start

There is structure to a wind-up in baseball. You see the pitcher pause, lift his leg and heave back his arm to thrust the ball forward. In a sermon introduction, there are also similar elements. As with a wind-up, a sermon introduction begins with a pause which draws attention. And as with a pitcher it need not be an inactive pause. Haddon W. Robinson has some excellent advice: "Nervousness occasionally makes the voice high and squeaky. Therefore, a preacher needs control, in order to speak his opening words in a composed, relaxed manner. Running the tongue to the back of the mouth or yawning with the mouth shut, which can be done while waiting to speak, reduces the tension in the throat. A deep breath before starting also puts the speaker at ease.''[1]

So start your introduction with an active pause.

Next, begin with three short sentences. The first couple of sentences of a sermon are often not heard by an audience because your audience needs some time to engage your sermon. Therefore, it is best to begin with three short sentences to fix the direction of your introduction in the minds of your listeners. Indeed, keep these sentences simple and sober, with few adjectives. In this way, these short sentences become sharp arrows implanted in the listener's brain.

After these opening sentences, use some unique method of laying the main movement before your congregation. These techniques will be discussed later in this chapter. But, the point is to direct the introduction of your main movement so that it grabs the attention of your listeners.

But, don't make this part of your introduction lengthy. Keep it brief. I actually don't watch too much baseball anymore just because it has become a slow-moving game. The pitcher can sometimes take a long time to wind up and deliver the pitch. That shouldn't happen in preaching. You should not spend so much time in winding up that the congregation is bored waiting for the pitch. With this in mind, a number of homiletic authors quote the elderly lady who told John Owen that he spent so long spreading the table that she lost her appetite for the meal.[2] So keep it brief! Don't make it any longer than 12 to 15 sentences. That won't always be possible if you are beginning with a story. But, the story and your comments about it should also be short. Without brevity, you will have too lengthy a wind up.

Your introduction also needs a good ending. When a pitcher throws, he snaps the ball firmly to his target. Introductions should also end with a snap. I usually conclude with a "snappy" direct statement of the main movement — where all your introductions should bring you if you are using the deductive method. Invariably, an introduction should close with a clear and concise statement of the main movement. If you are using the inductive method, the introduction will end with a distinct articulation of your first move.

Next, you make the longest pause of the sermon to give your congregation a moment to fix their focus before you move on.

So, the basic structure of your introduction should be a pause, a series of three-pointed sentences to prod the mind into action, a technique to present the main movement, an ending with a clear terse statement of the main movement and a concluding pause before entering the body of your message. The following is an example of such an introduction.

My brothers and sisters in the Lord Jesus Christ:

Today is World Hunger Sunday in our demonination. The World Relief Committee provides you with bulletin covers for this day. Also, in their packet of material they add the following portraits of World Hunger.

"Once again, after a day like so many others, a young mother in rural Bangladesh puts her children to bed. They are hungry. The small sum they and their mother earned weeding a neighbor's field bought only enough rice for one daily meal. Yet, a short distance away, in the landlord's warehouse, there is rice — great brimming baskets full, soon to be sold and shipped to the city.

A hardworking father in the Domician Republic bends down under the searing sun, swinging his machete against the tough sugarcane stalks. He can only dream of teaching the secrets of careful cultivation to his children. The land he works is part of a sugar plantation, and his wage for cutting cane is a dollar a day. He wonders whether his son, weakened by malnutrition, will survive to adulthood.

An elderly African returns from the mill with a meager sack of corn meal, the product of his lonely labor on the dusty sun-baked earth. He remembers when the land he farmed was green and the harvest of many sacks of grain was an occasion for a joyous family feast. But, that was before the land was divided, with the most fertile regions allotted to the powerful, and his people were forced to resettle.

In North America, an elderly widow ekes out a living on minimal government assistance. Before the end of the month, the money is gone. She eats dog food and uses little heat, so the gas isn't cut off."

I don't know about you, but such reports frustrate me deeply. I feel so helpless and so hopeless. I experience this World Hunger thing as a big burden!

But, one of the most comforting things I find about the Word of God is that it tells me I can do something about it!

I find that a tremendously comforting, indeed a liberating aspect about the Word of God. It tells me what I can do.

I want you to view the words of Scripture in our text this morning in that way as well. Not as burden, but as God's comforting, liberating direction of how to deal with the often hopelessly frustrating issue of world hunger.

"And what does the Lord require of you? To act justly and to love mercy and to walk humbly with your God?"

Praise God! He gives you some direction on how to deal with the plight of the poor.

In this sample introduction, the outlined structure is worked out. To make this structure function in your own sermons, see *The Moving Message Workbook*, Worksheet #4.

II. Principles For Moving Starts

The commonalities of a pitcher's wind up and an introduction in preaching are important to keep in mind when you form your moving start. These practices are the same as the three principles you followed in forming the main body of your message: activate, personalize and functionalize.

A. Activate

In baseball, the wind up provides the momentum for the ball's delivery. That's also how a sermon introduction should work, by building momentum to the main movement. The various techniques that can build momentum will be discussed below. But for now it is important to understand that introductions create thrust for the rest of the message. That is why I call introductions "Moving Starts."

But one caution. Don't be too fancy! That is something I discovered as a child pitching a tennis ball at a four- by eight-inch rectangle of insulbrick. My more fanciful wind ups were less successful. That can also happen in preaching. Your introduction can be so elaborate that you end up going off target. Once the sermon is rolling off track it is impossible to pull it back into focus without loosing the momentum of your message. Deliver a solid, sober introduction that hits the main movement right on. That will start the momentum.

As well, a fanciful introduction often promises far more than you can deliver. Don't pump up the congregation's hopes to a level that you can't possibly reach in your sermon. Baumann quotes one layman as saying to his pastor, "You started out by laying the foundation for a skyscraper, but you built a chicken coop upon it."[3]

But, there is reason for caution at the other end of the scale. Just as you shouldn't be arrogant and fanciful in your introduction, you shouldn't be a "wimp" either. Be solid, confident and direct in your wind up.

And another tip is to not apologize for your sermon in the introduction or anywhere, except maybe in personal conversation afterward. An apology does nothing for the momentum of your message. It throws the message out of gear, and at best, presents your congregation with a message that idles for 20 or 25 minutes. On this matter, Haddon W. Robinson says, "Through an apology a speaker hopes to win sympathy; at best he gains pity. A congregation will not be persuaded by that preacher. If you are unprepared, let the congregation discover it for themselves. In many cases they will never find out."[4]

So, in an introduction, build up momentum that's not too fancy or wimpy.

B. Personalize

In his World Series championship year of 1988, Los Angeles Dodgers star pitcher Orel Hershiser attributed his success to God and his personal computer. He said God gave him his talents and his computer helped him memorize the batting techniques of each of his opponenets. When a player came to the plate, Hershiser would concentrate momentarily on his batting skills and then pitch specifically for him.[5]

The same kind of personalized analysis is required for the wind up to a moving message. Know your audience and design a beginning that is specific to them.

It is always important to begin with your congregation. Jay E. Adams says, "Many pastors, instead, begin with the preaching portion. However, if the congregation is inattentive, does not know what the passage means, and what to look for in it, or can not see its relevance to anything that is taking place in their lives, the congregation needs orientation; it's better to begin with the congregation."[6]

So, begin with the congregation and lead them to the main movement.

Secondly, you should address a need of your congregation. With this piece of advice, Haddon W. Robinson says, "Sermons catch fire when flint strikes steel. When the flint of a person's problem strikes the steel of the Word of God, a spark ignites that burns in the mind."[7] Robert Schuller often uses the slogan, "Find a hurt and heal it!" We might say that in preaching you should, "Find a need and fill it!" (However, don't let your sermon content be controlled by human need. It should be governed by Scripture.) As you study Scripture and prepare your sermon, think seriously about the need the text addresses. And that need should rise to the surface of your introduction. In doing that you show your audience that you take them seriously. That will "fire them up" to listen.

For example, in the quoted introduction I addressed the frustration we all experience when confronted with the plight of the world's poor. We need to deal with that frustration. I draw that want to the surface and attempt to address it. You can personalize your introduction when you speak to a need in your congregation.

C. Functionalize:

In his wind up, the baseball pitcher forms the kind of ball that he is going to throw. But, he determines the pitch beforehand. The same goes for preaching. You must know your main movement and your moves before you construct the introduction. As Adams suggests, "While introductions may occur to you at any time during the preparation of a sermon, usually they are most easily and best developed when all else has been roughed in."[8]

When you have a clear understanding of the basic structure of your moving message, then design the introduction. Even though your introduction will introduce the sermon's main movement, it should not reveal the whole course of your sermon so your congregation can anticipate the rest of your message. Although your general purpose should be made clear in the introduction, always keep something hidden to keep your congregation engaged. The pitching parallel holds true again. When the pitcher winds up, everyone knows that his purpose is to throw the ball. But, he doesn't totally reveal his pitch in the wind up. The batter and the fans only know the nature of the pitch when the ball is on its way. This tension holds the batter's undivided attention and keeps the baseball fan glued to the action. The same principle remains in preaching an introduction. State your general purpose clearly, but always retain a tension about the specifics of your purpose until you say "Amen." If you do, the audience will stick with you to the "Amen" as well.

III. Technique

I am not that well versed in baseball, but I am certain that every pitcher has a variety of techniques for holding the ball in his fingers and swinging his arm, to form a specific pitch. In elementary school, I heard talk of fast balls and knuckle balls and the like. Just as there is an assortment of pitching techniques, there are many ways to form an introduction to engage your listeners in the momentum and purpose of your message. I will list a number of ways but only comment on them briefly since many are dealt with in other homiletics textbooks.

A. Paradox

A paradox exists when two conflicting ideas seem to be true. You can engage your audience with a paradox because the human mind will always struggle to resolve it. For example, the blessed can be unhappy and the suffering joyful. That paradox will immediately interest the minds of your listeners.

B. A Familiar Thought

A challenge to a familiar thought often grabs your audience's attention. They will usually take a position to oppose or accept the thought. As you preach they will intently debate with you. This challenge actively involves your audience in the flow of the message.

C. Rhetorical Question

There is nothing like a question to involve your listeners in the process of a sermon. When you ask a question, they must take responsibility for drawing a conclusion on what you are about to say. Like the two techniques above, it activates your hearers.

D. Statistics

Although there has been skepticism about their credibility, statistics have been a fad in preaching. But, a startling fact can be effective in engaging your hearers. Again, they will either support or discredit the fact. Your listeners then become involved in the activity of your message.

E. Humor

People like a joke. Although it can be engaging, a joke should be used with extreme caution. If you use humor, you have to be sure that it hits the content of your main movement dead on! If it doesn't, it will detract from the momentum and purpose of the message. Humor has a great danger of being too fancy and off target. It can also bring your whole message down to a level of triviality. Your listeners may feel that you are not serious about your message. This especially happens when your humor is beside the point. In order to avoid this "pitfall," your humor must hit the nail on the head.

F. A Story

Stories, if they are good, usually grab your audience immediately. They fall into three types. First, the impersonal story tells a "once upon a time" tale. Such a story tends to stimulate the imagination and cause the mental and emotional juices to flow.

Second, the personal story relates an instance from your own life. To develop a rapport with your congregation, a personal story helps them relate to your experience and message because it involves your listeners on a more personal level. There is one disadvantage; that the audience may focus more on you than on your main movement. Your audience then listens to you as if you are proclaiming your word, rather than God's Word.

Third, another method (that may be worth reviving) is the biblical story. Dr. T. Hoekstra in his book, *Gereformeerde Homiletiek*, suggests using scriptural stories that communicate that same basic point as your message.[9] About a half century ago, it was quite a popular way of introducing sermons with Dutch preachers. Dr. Louis Praamsma continued to use this method right up to his death in 1985, especially in his doctrinal sermons. His book on the Heidelberg Catechism, *Before The Face of God*, shows the practice of this method.[10]

Nobody can question the fact that the Bible tells moving and engaging stories. At your fingertips, you have a great resource of stories and illustrations. Sad to say, this source is so obvious that we often fail to take advantage of it. In his video *Drama in Speaking*, R. C. Sproul says there is an illustrative scripture story for every theme we preach on. This is just waiting to be used.[11]

Some people may object to this illustrative use of scripture. They feel perhaps, using God's Word in such a way lessens it authority. But, the Apostle Paul used scripture illustratively. In Galatians 4:21ff. he says, "Tell me, you who want to be under the law, are you not aware of what the law says? For it is written that Abraham had two sons, one by the slave woman and the other by the free woman. His son by the slave woman was born in the ordinary way; but his son by the free woman was born as the result of a promise. These things may be taken figuratively, for the women represent two covenants . . ." If Paul used the Bible illustratively, why can't you?

I hope to take more advantage of biblical stories in the future.

Conclusion

Working with all the structure, principles and techniques articulated in this chapter will be a bit difficult at first. It's like throwing a tennis ball at a four- by eight-inch rectangle of insulbrick from 30 feet out. But you, will find that with a bit of practice, you can "Whip out" some moving introductions. (See Worksheet 4.)

---

1. Haddon W. Robinson, *Biblical Preaching*, (Grand Rapids: Baker Book House, 1980), p. 166.
2. J. Daniel Baumann, *An Introduction to Contemporary Preaching*, (Grand Rapids: Baker Book House, 1972), p. 137.
3. Baumann, *An Introduction to Contemporary Preaching*, p. 138.
4. Robinson, *Biblical Preaching*, p. 165.
5. *Maclean's*, (Toronto: Maclean Hunter Limited, October 31, 1988), p. 44.
6. Jay E. Adams, *Preaching With Purpose*, (Grand Rapids, Zondervan Publishing House, 1982), p. 60.
7. Robinson, *Biblical Preaching*, p. 163.
8. Adams, *Preaching With Purpose*, p. 64.
9. T. Hoekstra, *Gereformeerde Homiletiek*, (Wageningen: Gebr. Zomer & Keuning's Uitgeversmaatschappij), p. 423.
10. Louis Praamsma, *Before The Face of God*, (Jordan Station, Ontario, Canada: Paideia Press Limited, 1987).
11. R. C. Sproul, *Drama in Speaking*, (Orlando, Florida: Ligonier Ministries, 1986), Video.

Chapter Nine

The Moving Stop

When I was a child, boxes of Kellogg's Corn Flakes contained special little "kiddie" prizes. One of the toys was a whirly-bird, a cylindrical stick with a plastic propeller on the one end. By rubbing the stick between your hands and with a quick flick, the whirly-bird would fly outward and upward, like a small helicopter in flight. The beaming faces of the children on the cereal box made the whirly-bird look so promising and exiting. But, as with most of these cereal-box toys, the poorly made toys didn't work well.

As a send-off for your message, the conclusion of a sermon should be like a whirly-bird. In order to fly, a conclusion requires attention to its structure, the principles of flight and a send-off technique. But, unlike cereal box toys, a conclusion is going to be effective only if well-constructed. As with the Moving Start, we also deal with the Moving Stop under the headings of structure, principles and techniques.

I. Structure Of The Moving Stop

The structure of a whirly-bird is very simple. There is nothing fancy about it, just a stick with a propeller on the end. And because of its simplicity, it flies. If you add "doo-dads" to a whirly-bird, it only creates drag and it is less likely to fly. So, also, the structure of a moving stop ought to be very simple, so your conclusion can fly.

Your conclusion should not be lengthy. Just as you wouldn't put a long stick on a whirly-bird because it adds more weight, so you should not make a long conclusion. It weighs down the ability of your message to fly in the lives of your listeners. A whirly-bird's stick is made just long enough for you to get your hands comfortably around it and give it a good send off. So make the conclusion of your sermon just the right length, to let the congregation grasp your message's main movement before you give it its final send-off.

You should be able to accomplish the conclusion in eight to 10 sentences. You will be more effective by creating a short conclusion which fixes the main movement in your congregations mind.

Your last sentence should be short and terse. Actually, you could end the whole sermon the same way you end a move. End with a series of three short sentences with the last being particularly sharp without adjectives or difficult clauses. That's the basic motion of a whirly-bird, rubbing it back and forth in your hands a few times before the final flick.

As well, it might be good to add a pause in the beginning of your conclusion. That will draw attention and prepare your audience for one last spin of the main movement.

Begin with a pause, give your main movement one short and simple final spin (by a technique suggested below) and send it off with three short terse sentences.

II. Principles For Moving Stop

While preparing a conclusion that will fly, there are certain principles to keep in mind, the recurring formula of activate, personalize, and functionalize.

A. Activate

Although conclusions are designed to end a sermon, you don't want the impact of your sermon to cease when you say, "Amen." So that your message will have some continuing effect, Hoekstra says conclusions should have an impact on the emotional and volitional life of your listeners.[1] That is why

I use the illustration of a whirly-bird when speaking of a conclusion. In some sense, the sermon shouldn't end when you give your main movement one last rub. It should begin to fly outward and upward in the lives of your listeners. Your message should have some lasting impact on their lives "out there" and in their relationship to the God "up there." In order to accomplish this, there has to be momentum to the conclusion to carry the sermon beyond its end. In short, you must have a moving stop.

You create this moving stop by portraying the Mover, Jesus Christ, as putting the spin in the main movement. Whatever the action in your main movement, Jesus at one time or another was also involved in a similar action on behalf of you and your audience. Let Him put the spin on your call to action. For example, if the action of your main movement is to seek justice, point to Christ's sacrifice was a fulfillment of God's justice for your sake. That gives biblical motivation and momentum to your call to justice.

After you have revealed Jesus as the Mover, give your main movement one last spin with a brisk send-off. Remember, your main movement has already been activated with its main verb in the active voice and in the present tense. When you give your main movement one last spin, you are building up the necessary momentum for a lasting impact.

There are, however, a few things to be noted. First, notice that you must give your main movement only one last spin and then let go. Do not touch it again! With a whirly-bird, you give it one last spin to send it off. If you touch it, the whirly-bird will flounder, lose its momentum and fall to the ground. Some speakers destroy the ongoing effect of their messages because they cling on to them. They spin their messages to death. Spin the main movement once and let go!

Also, you should not end your sermons in heaven for as Hoekstra points out, that takes away the sermon's lasting impact on "on earth lives."[2] But on the other hand, your conclusion should not be without heaven either. A purely horizontal message is burdensome and can leave your audience weighed down and struggling to move for the Lord. A conclusion, like a whirly-bird, must always head upward and outward. Depending on the direction you spin it, your message will go up and away from yourself or toward yourself. A conclusion, too, must simultaneously point your congregation upward to the forgiveness and strength they receive from God, and outward or inward to the responsibilities they have to the world and themselves. That forms a necessary balance. An only upward conclusion that gives part of the gospel will leave your hearers complacent. On the other hand, an only outward or inward ending leaves your listener powerless. End in heaven and on earth.

B. Personalize

You should end with your audience. Don't conclude with a subject but with some direct appeal to your congregation. A lecture ends with the subject, a sermon ends with the people. Broadus says, "The conclusion should be unmistakably personal in its aim."[3] This should happen quite naturally if you are using the main movement as the heart of your conclusion because it is already designed for a personal response to God.

C. Functionalize

While forming the main movement, you will have determined the purpose indicator (how, what, why, when, where, who). You should conclude in a way that is compatible with the purpose indicator of the sermon.

Also, looking at it from a functional perspective, it is important to end in a mood that harmonizes with the purpose of your sermon. That mood will also have been determined by the character of your main movement. For example, if your main movement is a Directive Divine Movement, it would be improper to end in an emotional manner. Such a movement is intended to motivate people to a specific action and emotion does not stimulate action. Therefore, in this instance it would be wise to conclude with an appeal to one's convictions rather than emotions.

Buttrick has some unique insights into this matter when he says, "What we have written may seem to go against a venerable pulpit tradition in which conclusions are designed for emotional impact or inspirational uplift. The tradition seems to be based on a Pietist assumption that feeling motivates. The assumption, unfortunately can not be supported; feeling may actually drain motivation. Long ago, the playwright Bertolt Brecht argued convincingly that "catharsis"* is the enemy of personal and social change. While "catharsis" may purge the soul, it may spend itself in emotion, and prompt no action at all."[4] So if you want to move people to action, don't conclude with great displays of emotion but with a sincere appeal to conviction. The congregation will not be moved by watching you emotionally "perform." They will only be moved by your genuine address to their convictions.

Conversely, if your main movement is an Exclamatory Worship Movement, it is better to direct your conclusion at the emotions rather than the convictions of your listeners. By so doing, you will stir the hearts of your hearers to genuine worship.

Actually, if you are true to your main movement, and give it one last spin in your conlcusion, then all of this should flow from your message. The purpose indicator and mode of the main movement will permeate the conclusion so that you will be pinning the tail on the right donkey. There will be a natural harmony between the body of your sermon and its conclusion.

But, to arrive at the desired intention and purpose for any message, it is important to end positively. In the body of your

*Catharsis is the purging of an audience's emotions.

message you may point out the ridiculousness of a certain attitude or behavior. But, you should always end with a positive alternative. Broadus quotes C.S. Patton as saying, "Negative statements belong in the early part of the sermon. These may often be very important. We teach by contrast. It is frequently necessary to clear the ground before one can put up his own structure; but one should not still be clearing ground in his concluding sentences or bring in at that place things which he wants to warn his hearers away from."[5] The Heidelberg Catechism provides a good example of this technique. When it addresses each of the commandments, it begins by speaking out against certain behavior, but ends by pointing you to a positive alternative.[6] So, always end with a positive enunication of your purpose. End positively!

To sum up this principle: let the purpose and mood of the main movement govern the form of your conclusion so it ends with a positive expression of your message.

III. Techniques For Creating A Moving Stop

In my childhood experience, I have discovered certain techniques to send a whirly-bird flying. I was always a "klutzy" sort of kid, whose hands were all thumbs. Therefore, the poor performance of the whirly-birds could be attributed as much to my lack of technique as to the cheapness of the toy. There are also valuable techniques you can learn to make your conclusion fly.

A. Rehearsal Of The Moves

This method briefly rehearses the moves of the sermon. It may be somewhat didactic, but I avoid sounding schoolish by placing distinctive images from each move in a series of short sentences. At the end of this chapter, there is an illustration of this technique. This kind of conclusion is for obvious reasons an appropriate ending to sermons in the Deductive Didactic Style.

B. Returning To The Introduction

If you have left some issue unresolved in the introduction and have only addressed it from a distance in the body of sermon, then it is wise to confront the issue in the conclusion. Your listeners deserve that much. If your audience discovers you have a habit of leaving loose ends, they won't be bothered to stay with you in the future.

C. Quotation, Story, Poem, Or Hymn

All of these methods can bring the main movement to the mind of your listeners one last time. But, you have to be sure that your quotation, story, poem or hymn hits the content of the main movement dead on. Close is not good enough, because it will throw everything out of focus. And what you were trying to convey will soon be forgotten. But, a quotation, story, poem, or hymn that hits the point of your message can work effectively to fix it in the memory of your listeners.

D. Personal Testimony

This can also be very effective provided your testimony directly addresses the main movement. But, a personal testimony has the added difficulty of putting the audience's focus on the preacher, not the gospel. When you give a personal testimony remember that the story is not about you, but about how the truth of the Word of God is active in your life.

E. "Altar" Calls

These can be very effective conclusions to evangelistic-type sermons which try to motivate people to step forward and accept Christ as their Lord and Savior. If done properly, they have their time and place, as a clear call of the gospel. "Altar" calls must appeal to the whole person, to both heart and mind. A call elicits not just an emotional reaction from the listener, but rather a holistic response to God's grace.

F. Doxology

If your main movement has, as its main purpose, the motivation of your audience to praise, then a doxology would be a good primer for a response from your hearers. That is particularly appropriate in sermons on the praise psalms.

An illustration of a moving stop using a rehearsal of moves follows. It comes from the same World Hunger sermon mentioned in the previous chapter that is based on Micah 6:8.

This is, for me anyway, a tremendously encouraging, comforting direction from God's Word in the midst of my frustration with world hunger.

You have seen the pictures of starving children, too, I'm sure. They are on television and in magazines. It makes my soul cry out, "What can I do?"

God gives you and me some liberating Words.

Seeing that your Savior sacrificed himself to fulfill God's justice for you, seek justice for the poor.

Seeing that it pleased God to give his son for your salvation, consider it a pleasure to share with the poor.

Seeing how God sent his son from heaven to have solidarity with you, seek to walk in humility and hope with your God and the poor.

Share your food with the others at the global table. Get a kick out of it! And walk in solidarity with God and the poor in humility and hope. Amen.

This conclusion does it all. It clearly presents the Mover, and in the light of His power gives the main movement one last spin. It ends with three short statements. It is a conclusion that will send the message onward and upward in the lives of your listeners even after the closing. "Amen." (See Work Sheet #5 of *The Moving Message Workbook*.)

---

1. T. Hoekstra, *Gereformeerde Homiletiek*, (Wageningen: Gebr, Zomer & Keuning's Uitgeversmaatschappij), p. 427.

2. Ibid.

3. John A. Broadus, *On The Preparation and Delivery of Sermons*, revised by Vernon L. Stanfield, (San Francisco: Harper and Row Publishers, 1979), p. 110.

4. David Buttrick, *Homiletic*, (Philadelphia: Fortress Press, 1987), p. 108.

5. Broadus, *On Preparation and Delivery of Sermons*, p. 117.

6. *Ecumenical Creeds and Reformed Confessions*, (Grand Rapids: Board of Publications of The Christian Reformed Church, 1979), p. 45-55.

CONCLUSION

If I know you well — and I think I do, because I am like you — most of you will react to this book with some degree of disgust. In fact, two of my respondents who gave my system a "dry run" were very upset. I suspect that a few others didn't complete the evaluation form for a similar reason. They said they didn't send it back because it was too much work to fit it into their busy schedules. But, I suspect they found this book too bothersome.

Maybe it's the emphasis on order and structure that repulses you. But, Glen C. Knecht, refers to order as, "Heaven's First Love." He says that in creation God built his world according to his own order. A sense of order is built right into the nature of things even from such phrases as "the evening and the morning were the first day." The predictability of the creation, the rhythmic movement of the heavenly bodies, and the change of seasons are reminders of the God of design.[1] A preacher, who loves his hearers as God loves his children in Jesus Christ, will also design his sermonic creations with a love for order.

But the real reason for your discontent may be the same as the lady's reaction mentioned in the third chapter. She was troubled by my sermons because she found the approach of them too direct. I think she has a point. But, I suspect there was another reason for her annoyance; what she heard was too painful. That may be the reason for your discontent as well.

I readily admit that, even though in the method of sermon preparation set forth in this book is simple and easy to follow, it is painful! But, I have discovered that nothing worthwhile in life comes easy. The aphorism, "No pain, no gain," popularized by Robert Schuller, holds true. There is no spiritual growth without pain. And, there is no progress in developing preaching skills without pain. M. Scott Peck in his book, *The Road Less Traveled*, quotes Benjamin Franklin as saying, "Those things that hurt instruct," and goes on to say,

"Therefore let us inculcate in ourselves and our children the means for achieving mental and spiritual health. By this, I mean let us teach ourselves and our children the necessity for suffering and the value thereof, the need to face problems directly and to experience the pain involved."[2] Our North American culture has not prepared us for that. Philip Yancy writes, "The well-known German Pastor and theologian Helmut Thielicke was once asked what was the greatest problem he had observed in the United States. He replied, 'They have an inadequate view of suffering.' "[3] We have been programmed to think that all pain is bad and we must avoid it at all costs. If you are going to benefit from this book you have to make a choice to accept and experience the pain that accompanies it. But you and I have a reason to take such pain upon ourselves. That reason is Jesus Christ! He bore the pain of the cross for you and I. Indeed, he took the pain of God's accumulated wrath upon himself for the sins of the whole human race. The pain of structuring your message is but a small token of thanksgiving which pales in the face of his suffering. May the spirit of God go with you.

---

1. Glen C. Knecht, "Sermon Structure and Flow," *The Preacher and Preaching, ed, Samuel T. Logan, Jr.,* (Phillipsburg, New Jersey: Presbyterian and Reformed Publishing Company, 1986), p. 276.
2. M. Scott Peck, *The Road Less Traveled,* (New York: Simon and Schuster, 1978), p. 16, 17.
3. Philip Yancy, *Open Windows,* (Westchester, Illinois: Crossway Books, 1982), p. 73.

APPENDIX I

Understanding The Text

A. After you have determined the original reading of the text, use lexicons and grammars to help you make your own translation of the text! Pay careful attention to the moods, tenses, etc., of the verbs, and to the gender, number, and case of the nouns. Observe every part of speech and note its function. Compare your translation with translations in every language in which you have competence. Try to grasp the reasons for difference.

B. Consider the original circumstances of the text and try to grasp the original intention of the author. Try to understand what the original recipients of the revelation understood by it. Use reliable works on Old and New Testament Introduction and at least two good commentaries, in order to deepen your understanding of the text. Even at this point you should begin to feel how the message moves beyond its historical setting to your congregation.

C. Read and re-read the text in its broad context until the central thrust of the text becomes evident.

D. When you think you have heard the central message of the text, try to put this down in one, clear sentence. Read parallel passages in which the same truth is taught, being sensitive to the significance of differences in formulation! Keep asking, "What is God saying in my text?" The key to sound preaching is understanding the revelatory intention of the text!

Dr. Carl Kromminga, "Making The Reconstructive Sermon," Class Notes, January 1988.

THE MOVING MESSAGE WORKBOOK CONTENTS

Work Sheet 1
Constructing A Main Movement

Step 1: State the theme of the text in one simple sentence.

____

Step 2: Activate the theme. Make sure the statement is a complete sentence with a verb, in the active voice and the present tense.

____

Step 3: Personalize the theme. Rewrite the statement in terms of "God" and "you."
"God ____________ you ______________________"

Step 4: Functionalize the Theme. Determine the purpose indicator (PI.) and write it up accordingly. (How, what, why, when, where, or who) (See as follows)

How?

"God ____________ you ________ BY ______________"
(verb) **(answer to PI. how?)**

What? Who?
"God ____________ you ______ ABOUT ______________"
(verb) **(answer to PI. what?)**

Why?
"God ____________ you ____ BECAUSE ______________"
(verb) **(answer to PI. why?)**

When?
"God ____________ you ______ BEFORE ______________"
(verb) **(answer to PI. when?)**

Where?
"God ________ you ________ TO ____________________"
(verb) (answer to PI. where?)

CLEAR STATEMENT OF THE MAIN MOVEMENT:

____

Step 5: Determine the mood and direction of the passage and construct the main movement accordingly. (See Table 1)

A. From the table choose the kind of movement that best represents the mood and direction of your Bible passage.
B. Look up the page reference with the type of movement you choose and read up on its characteristics.
C. Write up the main movement according to the type that you have chosen from the table.

COMPLETED MAIN MOVEMENT:

____

Work Sheet 2
The Moves

Step 1: Write down what you believe to be the main thoughts of the scripture passage.

____

____

____

____

____

Step 2: Take three or four of the main thoughts and activate, personalize and functionalize them.

I. God __________ you ____________________
(verb of MM.*) **(first part of answer to PI.)**

II. God ______ you ____________________
(verb of MM.) **(second part of answer to PI.)**

III. God ____ you ____________________
(verb of MM.) **(third part of answer to PI.)**

Step 3: Write the moves into a progressive conversational sentence using conjunctions from Table 2 to ensure there is a proper flow to your message. (See p. 120 of The Moving Message)

____

____

____

____

Step 4: Rewrite the moves in point form as in Step 2 prefacing each of them with the conjunction or transitional phrase by which they are prefaced in your conversational sentence.

I. God ________________ you ________________

**Indicates Main Movement*

II. _______ God _______ you ________________

III. _______ God _______ you ________________

(As the textbook indicates, this will help you to make natural transitions from one move to the next.)

Step 5: Determine what form or style you want your sermon to take. See Figure 1 to get a more concrete representation of these options. See Table 3 to determine the form and style that is best suited to your text.

A. From the table above choose the form and style that best represents the form and style of your text.
B. Look up the page reference with the kind of style you choose and read up on its characteristics.
C. Re-structure the form of your sermon in Step 4 of Work Sheet 2 to represent the choice that you have made above.

____

____

____

____

____

Work Sheet 3
Developing The Move

Main Movement:

____

Introduction:

I. First Move:

____

Opener: (Short punchy articulation of your move)

A. Theology

1. ____

2. ____

3. ____

B. Oppositions

1. ____

2. ____

3. ____

C. Experience

1. ____

2. ____

3. ____

Closer: (Short punchy statement of your main move, possibly using the "pause, punch, pause" method)

II. Second Move:

____

Opener: (Short punchy articulation of your move)

A. Oppositions

B. Experience

C. Theology

Closer: (Short punchy statement of your main move, possibly using the "pause, punch, pause" method)

III. Third Move:

____

Opener: (Short punchy articulation of your move)

A. Experience

B. Oppositions
C. Theology
Closer: (Short punchy statement of your main move, possibly using the ''pause, punch, pause'' method)
Conclusion:

Work Sheet 4
Constructing The Moving Start

I. Active pause . . .

II. Three short statements in order to get your audience engaged in your message.

____

____

____

III. Use one of the following methods to place the main movement before your listeners.

A. Paradox ____
B. Familiar thought ____
C. Rhetorical Question ____
D. Statistics ____
E. Humor ____
F. Impersonal Story ____
G. Personal Story ____
H. Biblical Story ____

____

____

____

____

IV. A clear and crisp statement of the main movement.

____

V. The longest pause of the sermon.

Work Sheet 5
Constructing The Moving Stop

I. Pause . . .

II. Statement of how Christ himself fulfilled the action of the main movement.

____
____
____
____
____

III. Give the main movement one more spin using one of the following techniques. End the technique with clear statement of the main movement.

A. Rehearsal of The Moves ____
B. Returning To The Introduction ____
C. Quotation, Song, Poem, Hymn ____
D. Personal Testimony ____
E. Altar Calls ____
F. Doxology ____

____
____
____
____

main movement

IV. Close with three short terse statements.

____
____
____

The Mover

At this point, determine where you will explicitly mention Jesus Christ as the Mover of your message. (The Moving Start, one of the moves, the Moving Stop.) Put an asterisk by it in your outline. Remember, your listeners want to see Jesus. (See Page 77 in The Moving Message.)

TABLE 1

DETERMINING THE MOOD AND DIRECTION OF THE MAIN MOVEMENT

	DIVINE MOVEMENTS		WORSHIP MOVEMENTS	
	Biblical Literature	Desired Response	Biblical Literature	Desired Response
Declarative	narrative parable miracle promises of God (see p. 33)	trust confidence assurance	Confessional Psalms and other confessional literature (see p. 42)	affirmation of one's faith in God
Directive	commands prophetic directives directives from the Gospels admonishments of the Epistles (see p. 35)	specific action	Prayer Psalms prayers (see p. 44)	prayerful response
Exclamatory	Hosea Gospel of John Epistles of John apocalyptic literature (Ezekiel, Daniel, Revelation) (see p. 37)	stir the emotions emotional response of fear, sorrow, love or joy	Praise Psalms (see p. 46)	praise response
Interrogative	Laments of God Questioning by God (see p. 38)	contemplation introspection meditation self-examination	Lament Psalms Wisdom Psalms Wisdom Literature (see p. 47)	response of lament resulting in vindication of God
Conditional	Proverbs (see p. 39)	a response of prudent well-advised action	Contrary to fact conditions on God (see p. 48)	affirmation of the goodness and graciousness of God

NOTE: The table indicates which kind of movement is best suited to a certain type of biblical literature and the intended response of your listeners

TABLE 2
CONJUNCTIONS FOR PROGRESSIVE CONVERSATIONAL SENTENCES*

Coordinate Conjunctions:	and, but, for, yet, nor, so
Correlative Conjunctions:	either-or, neither-nor, both-and, not only-but also
Subordinate Conjunctions:	after, although, as, because, before, for, if, since, than, though, unless, until, when, where, while
Phrasal Conjunctions:	as if, as well, provided that, in order that, so that, as though, rather than

TABLE 3
DETERMINING THE STYLE AND FORM OF THE SERMON

	Deductive	Inductive
Narrative		Biblical Narrative Miracles and Parables
Didactic	Epistles Proverbs Ecclesiasties other teaching passages	
Aesthetic	Some Psalms	Prophets Revelation Psalms

* *A. W. McGuirre, Grammar is Important, (Agincourt, Ontario: The Book Society Limited, 1949), p. 125-128.*

FIGURE 1

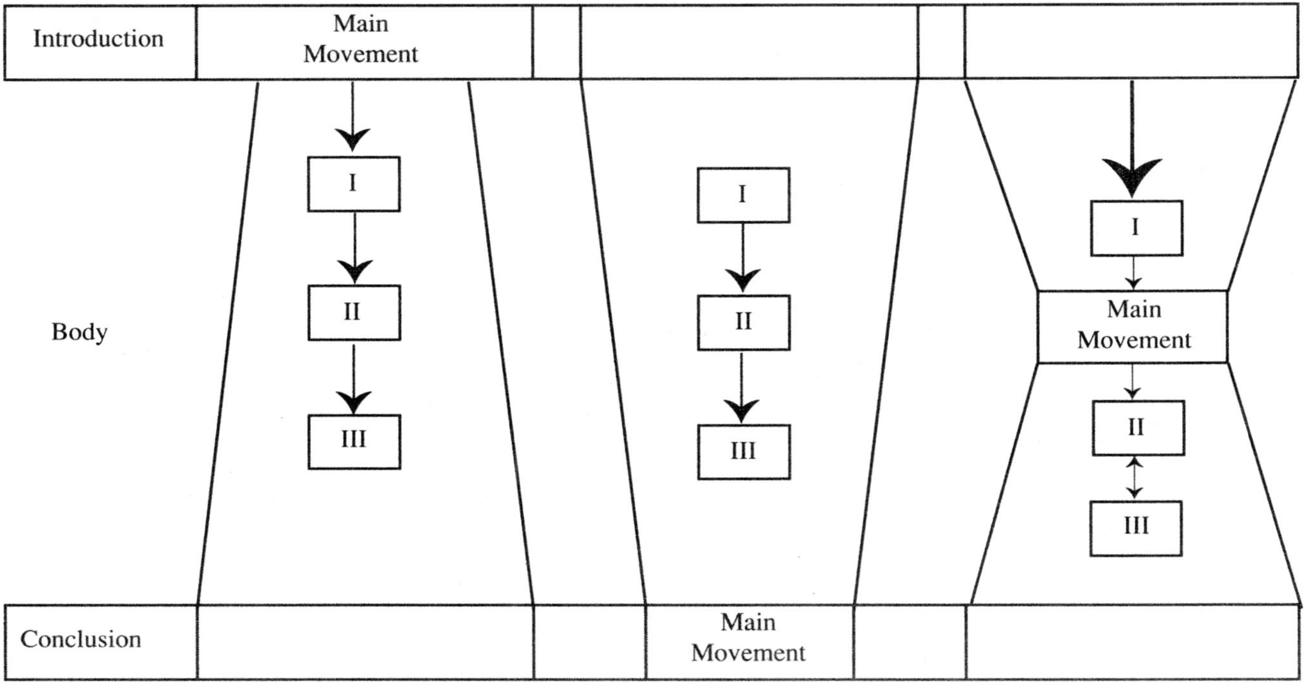
Deductive Development
Inductive Development
Inductive-Deductive Development
Introduction
Main Movement
I
II
III
I
II
III
I
Main Movement
II
III
Body
Conclusion
Main Movement

Bibliography

Adams, Jay E. *Preaching With Purpose*, Grand Rapids: Zondervan Publishing House, 1982.

Aho, Gerhard. *The Lively Skeleton: Thematic Approches and Outlines*, St. Louis: Concordia Publishing House, 1977.

Alter, Robert. *The Art Of Biblical Narrative*, New York: Basic Books Inc., 1981.

Anderson, Bernhard. *Out of the Depths*, Philadelphia: Westminster Press, 1974.

Archer Jr., Gleason L. *Survey of Old Testament Introduction*, Chicago: Moody Press, 1977.

Baird, John E. *Preparing For Pulpit and Platform*, Nashville/New York: Abingdon Press, 1968.

Baumann, J. Daniel. *An Introduction to Contemporary Preaching*, Grand Rapids: Baker Book House, 1972.

Bolhofner, Mark. *Evangelistic Preaching in The Local Church*, Doctor of Ministry Project, 1988. (unpublished)

Broadus, John A. *On the Preparation and Delivery of Sermons*, revised by Vernon L. Stanfield, San Francisco: Harper & Row Publishers, 1979.

Buttrick, David. *Homiletic*. Philadelphia: Fortress Press, 1987.

Davis, H. Grady. *Design For Preaching*. Philadelphia: Fortress Press, 1958.

Dijk, K. *De Dienst Der Prediking*. Kampen, The Netherlands: J. H. Kok, 1955.

Ecumenical Creeds and Reformed Confessions. Grand Rapids: Board of Publications of The Christian Reformed Church, 1979.

Edwrds, O. C. Jr. *Elements of Homoletic*. New York: Pueblo Publishing Company, 1982.

Fee, Gordon D. and Stuart, Douglas. *How To Read The Bible For All That It's Worth*. Grand Rapids: Zondervan Pub. House, 1982.

Greidanus, Sidney. *Sola Scriptura*. Toronto: Wedge Publishing Foundation, 1970.

Greidanus, Sidney. *The Modern Preacher and The Ancient Text*. Grand Rapids: William B. Eerdmans Publishing Company, 1988.

Hoekstra, T. *Gereformeerde Homiletiek*. Wageningen, The Netherlands: Gebr. Zomer & Keuning's Uitgeversmaatschappij.

Knecht, Glen C. "Sermon Structure and Flow." *The Preacher and Preaching.*, ed. Samuel T. Logan Jr. Phillipsburg, New Jersey: Presbyterian and Reformed Publishing Company, 1986.

Kromminga, Carl. "Making The Reconstructive Sermon." *Class Notes*. January 1988.

Lewis, Ralph L. *Inductive Preaching*. With Gregg Lewis. Westchester Illinois: Crossway Books, 1983.

Maclean's, Toronto: Maclean Hunter Limited, October 31, 1988.

McGuirre, A. W. *Grammar is Important*. Agincourt, Ontario: The Book Society Limited, 1949.

Peck, M. Scott. *The Road Less Traveled*. New York: Simon and Schuster, 1978.

Perry, Lloyd M. *Biblical Preaching for Today's World*. Chicago: Moody Press , 1973.

Praamsma, Louis. *Before The Face of God*. Jordan Station, Ontario, Canada: Paideia Press Limited, 1987.

Quirk, Randolph; Greenbaum, Sidney; Leech, Geoffrey; and Svartvik, Jan. *A Comprehensive Grammar of The English Language*. New York: Longman Inc., 1985.

Report 31, "Capital Punishment Study Committee," *Acts of Synod of the Christian Reformed Church in North America*. Grand Rapids: Board of Publications of the Christian Reformed Church, 1981.

Robinson, Haddon W. *Biblical Preaching*. Grand Rapids: Baker Book House, 1980.

Ryken, Leland. *Literature of The Bible*. Grand Rapids: Zondervan Pub. House, 1974.

Sproul, R. C. "Drama in Speaking." *How to Grow Your Church*. Orlando, Florida: Ligonier Ministries, 1986. (video)

Straatsma, A. K. "Niet Gij, Maar Wij." *Hoe Vindt U Dat Er Gepreekt Moet Worden*? ed. A. G. Barkey Wolf. Zwolle, The Netherlands: La Riviere & Voorhoeve.

Sweazey George E. *Preaching The Good News*. Englewood Cliffs, New Jersey: Prentice-Hall, Inc., 1976.

Tan, Paul Lee. *Encyclopedia of 7700 Illustrations*. Rockville, Maryland: Assurance Publishers, 1979.

Wood, Charles R. *Sermon Outlines for Special Days and Occasions*. Grand Rapids: Kregel Publications, 1970.

Yancy, Philip. *Open Windows*. Westchester, Illinois: Crossway Books, 1982.